Concepts in the Social Sciences

Series Editor: Frank Parkin

Published Titles

Concepts in the Social Sciences

Bureaucracy

Second Edition

David Beetham

Open University Press
Buckingham

Open University Press
Celtic Court
22 Ballmoor
Buckingham
MK18 1XW

First edition published 1987. Reprinted 1993

First published in this second edition 1996

A catalogue record of this book is available from the British Library

ISBN 0 335 19654 3 (pb)   0 335 19655 1 (hb)

Typeset by Type Study, Scarborough

Printed and bound by CPI Group (UK) Ltd, Croydon, CR0 4YY

Contents

Preface to the Second Edition

The distinctive argument and inter-disciplinary perspective of the first edition have been maintained in this second one, but both text and bibliography have been fully updated in the light of academic and political developments since 1987. I am grateful to Vicki Harvey for help in compiling the revised bibliography and guide to further reading.

David Beetham

Introduction

Bureaucracy is something we all love to hate. It presents simultaneously the contradictory images of bungling inefficiency and threatening power. Incompetence, red tape and feather-bedding on the one side; manipulation, obstructionism and Byzantine intrigue on the other: there is almost no evil that has not at some point been debited to its account. Bureaucracy has the rare distinction of being anathematized across the political spectrum. The Right seeks to limit it in the name of the free market; the Centre to reform it in the name of openness and accountability; the Left to replace it in the name of participation and self-management. Yet it displays an impressive capacity to resist all such encroachments. 'The dictatorship of the official is on the advance', wrote Max Weber, bureaucracy's most distinguished theoretician. This was, he argued, because of its unique capacity to handle the complex administrative tasks of a mass industrial society. Necessary, but persistently problematic: this is the paradox with which bureaucracy seems to confront us.

But what exactly is bureaucracy? The student whose interest is aroused by declamatory opening paragraphs like the above tends to be quickly thrown into a state of confusion as he or she penetrates deeper into the subject. The confusion arises from the many different meanings that have been assigned to the term bureaucracy, of which the following is by no means an exhaustive list: rule by officials, a system of professional administration, organizational inefficiency, public administration, a non-market institution, undemocratic organization. In the face of this variety of usages, writers on bureaucracy tend to adopt one of two definitional strategies. The first is a prescriptive approach; they declare confidently that bureaucracy really means public administration, or organizational inefficiency, or whatever, as the case may be. This approach avoids confusion, but only so long as the student does not read anyone else's work. The second approach is a more descriptive and agnostic one, whereby the writer explores the very different meanings that have been given to the term, and concludes, perhaps regretfully, that there is really no such thing as bureaucracy at all: only a cluster of quite different phenomena, tenuously related to one another, to which a common name has misleadingly become attached. This approach certainly helps sort out the confusion, but only at the expense of dissolving bureaucracy as a unified subject of enquiry. At this point the student may feel a bit let down: does bureaucracy, then, not really exist after all?

The approach I adopt in this book is different from either of these. I argue that there is indeed an identifiable subject of enquiry, called bureaucracy, though it occurs in different forms; and that there is a recurrent set of concerns about it which relate to the problems of bureaucratic efficiency and bureaucratic power. However, we can only attain a coherent definition of bureaucracy, and an adequate understanding of it, by analysing the different perspectives from which it has been treated, and by exploring their relationship to one another. Only a critical analysis, of the major different approaches to bureaucracy, will enable us to reach a systematic and conclusive understanding of it, that neither elevates one aspect into the whole, nor dissolves the whole into a multiplicity of disconnected elements.

A useful strategy to adopt whenever we come across different or disputed definitions of a term in the social sciences is to ask two questions. What is the term being *contrasted with* in each case? What perspective and set of problems is this contrast designed to emphasize? If we ask these two questions about the term bureaucracy, we shall quickly discover that the different definitions are not arbitrary or haphazard, but derive their significance from the context of different academic disciplines: comparative government, the sociology of organization, public administration and political economy respectively. To understand the concept of bureaucracy, in other words, is first of all to understand the different uses to which it has been put within the particular social sciences. Let me take each of these in turn.

The standard usage of the term bureaucracy in the nineteenth century was to indicate a type of political system, literally 'rule by the bureau'. It denoted a system in which ministerial positions were occupied by career officials, usually answerable to a hereditary monarch. Bureaucracy was contrasted with a system of representative government, i.e. the rule of elected politicians accountable to a representative assembly or parliament. Thus J.S. Mill, for example, in his classic work *Representative Government*, considered bureaucracy as the only serious alternative to a representative system, and he assessed the characteristic advantages and disadvantages of each. In the twentieth century, bureaucratic rule is as likely to be a feature of military dictatorship, one-party government or other forms of authoritarian rule as it is of hereditary monarchy, but the contrast with parliamentary democracy still applies. It is a contrast that belongs to the discipline of comparative government, and its concern to explore the distinctive differences in character and functioning between different political systems.

A second usage belongs to the sociology of organization, and derives originally from the work of Max Weber. To Weber bureaucracy meant, not a type of government, but a system of administration carried out on a continuous basis by trained professionals according to prescribed rules. Weber noted how this type of administration, although originating in bureaucratic states such as Prussia, was becoming increasingly prevalent in all political systems, representative as well as monarchical, and indeed in all organizations where complex and large-scale administrative tasks were undertaken: business enterprises, trade unions, political parties, etc. This very general concept of bureaucracy as professional administration embodies a double contrast: first, between administration and policy making, which is the responsibility of the association that employs the bureaucracy, and to which it is legally subordinate; secondly, between modern and traditional methods of administration, which are arranged on non-professionalized lines. This general concept belongs to the sociology of organization, with its concern to understand the most general characteristics and types of organization in modern societies.

A third usage derives from the discipline of public administration. As the term implies, bureaucracy here means *public* administration as opposed to administration within a private organization. The point of the contrast is to identify the differences between the two and to emphasize the qualitatively different character that a system of administration possesses by virtue of its situation within the field of government, such as its compulsory character, its particular relation to the law, its concern with a general rather than a private interest, the public accountability of its operations, and so on. From the standpoint of this discipline, in comparison with the sociology of organization, what distinguishes different types of professional administration is as significant as what they have in common.

A fourth usage derives from political economy. At first sight it looks the same as the previous one, because it overlaps considerably with it. However, as the name of the discipline implies, it is concerned with distinguishing organizations in economic terms, according to the source of their revenue. From this standpoint a bureaucracy is defined as a non-market organization, which is financed by means of a general grant from its parent association, in contrast to one that is financed by the sale of its product on the market. Although the majority of such organizations are to be found in the public sphere, there are many that are not (e.g. churches, charities, voluntary associations), while, on the other hand, some government bodies sell their products on the market (railway companies, car manufacturers, etc.), and are thus not technically bureaucracies. The purpose of defining bureaucracy in this way is to emphasize that the character and mode of operation of an organization varies systematically according to the method of its financing, and the economic environment in which it operates.

Each of these disciplinary standpoints produces its own definition of bureaucracy, and its own point of contrast with the non-bureaucratic, according to its distinctive preoccupation and focus of interest. The starting point for understanding the subject of bureaucracy, therefore, is with an understanding of these different disciplines. The first chapter will concern itself with three of these – the sociology of organization, political economy and public administration – and with clarifying the differences between their approaches to bureaucracy. Underlying the differences, however, certain common themes and preoccupations will emerge: a concern to define the meaning of administrative efficiency, and to specify the conditions for its realization; to assess how far bureaucracy meets these conditions; to understand how bureaucracies function in practice, and how the manner of their functioning affects organizational goals and policies, to which the administration is supposedly subordinate. Although their accounts differ from, and at points contradict, one another, they are nevertheless capable, after critical analysis, of being integrated into a more inclusive definition of bureaucracy and theory of its working.

However, what the disciplines considered in Chapter 1 can contribute to our understanding of bureaucracy, while important, is necessarily limited. This is not only because, like bureaucracy itself, their strength as academic disciplines derives from the division of labour, with its fragmentation of knowledge. It is also that, even when taken together, their perspective is confined to the study of bureaucracy as a self-contained entity, to be understood from within, and in isolation from both history and society at large. The questions that preoccupy them – how bureaucracies function, and how they might do so more efficiently – are essentially those of the manager or administrator transposed into a context of academic enquiry. Nor is this accidental. The academic disciplines of public administration, and the economics and sociology of organization, have grown up in close association with the practice of administration, whether in government, business, or society at large, and with the education of those who will occupy bureaucratic positions in these spheres. It is not surprising, therefore, that they share both the insights and the limitations of such a perspective.

In order to move beyond the issues of bureaucratic functioning and efficiency, to an analysis of bureaucratic power and its expansion over the course of the twentieth century, it is necessary to adopt the perspective of a historical sociology. In Chapter 2 I consider two of the main competing paradigms of historical sociology and their respective analyses and critiques of bureaucratic power. The first is Weberian political sociology, with its location of bureaucracy at the centre of the modernization process, its analysis of the source of its power in the monopoly of knowledge and organization, and its distinctively liberal concern about the expansion and concentration of this power within the political domain. The second school of historical sociology is Marxist political economy, with its location of bureaucracy in a theory of capitalist development, its analysis of power as constituted by the ownership and control of the means of production, and its definition of bureaucracy as the form of administration characteristic of a class-divided society. Consideration of these theories will lead us not only into the wider themes of comparative government, but into discussions about the nature of the former Soviet Union, and whether alternatives to capitalism must necessarily degenerate into a form of bureaucratic rule.

Where the standpoints of Chapter 1 treat bureaucracy from within, those of Chapter 2 treat it from without. The Weberian perspective represents that of the liberal, non-bureaucratic élites, who see their social independence threatened by the expansion of bureaucracy, which they seek to constrain through strategies of institutional pluralism, and control by individual leadership from above. The Marxist perspective represents that of the working class, who are subordinate to bureaucratic authority in both economy and state, and who seek to transform it through collective action from below. In the third and final chapter I shall offer a critical synthesis of these different accounts of bureaucracy within a more philosophical mode of discourse, and from the standpoint of a democratic theory that requires for its completeness both an understanding of bureaucratic operation and the conditions for administrative efficiency, and an analysis of bureaucratic power, incorporating both liberal and Marxist insights. From this standpoint, and this standpoint alone, I shall argue, it is possible to reach a conclusive definition and systematic understanding of bureaucracy.

The theme of this book, then, is that to construct an adequate theory of bureaucracy is, first, to situate the various definitions of the concept within the context of particular social sciences, and to identify their relationship to one another; it is, next, to engage with the main competing perspectives or paradigms of historical sociology and political theory; it is, finally, to understand the relationship of all these in turn to the outlook and practical interests of major social groupings. These are not optional and unnecessary deviations from the main enquiry. They constitute essential and successive steps in the systematic search for an adequate theory of bureaucracy. And, if I am right, the result of the search will be an understanding, not of bureaucracy alone, but of the nature of social science itself.

1
Models of
Bureaucracy

Introduction

The purpose of this chapter is to explore the models of bureaucracy
developed within different academic disciplines. What is a model
for? People who talk about models in social science often confuse
three quite different purposes which the construction of a model can
serve: to provide a *definitional* test; to set a *normative* standard; to
develop an *explanatory* framework. A definitional model of bureaucracy will be concerned to specify the criteria which determine
what is to count as a bureaucracy, and what is not. It answers the
question: how do we recognize a bureaucracy when we see one? A
normative model seeks to prescribe what are the necessary conditions for organizational efficiency or effectiveness, and to explore
how far bureaucracy (either in general or in particular) is able to
satisfy these conditions. It answers the question: how efficient are
bureaucracies? An explanatory model aims to provide a framework
for explaining the way bureaucracies function in practice, and why
they have the consequences they do for the formation and execution
of policy. It answers the question: why do bureaucracies function as
they do?

Now of course these different questions are interrelated. To
answer the question about bureaucratic efficiency, we need to know
how bureaucracies actually work; and a typical reason for finding
out why bureaucracies function as they do, is to discover how they
might be made more efficient, and what are the major limitations or
obstacles to doing so. But the fact that the three types of question –
definitional, normative and explanatory – are interrelated, does not

make them the same question, and we need first of all to distinguish them in order to understand their interconnection. Those writers who *define* bureaucracy as organizational efficiency or inefficiency are confusing two different questions that need to be kept apart. And a similar mistake is made by those who assume that a normative model of 'rational' decision making will suffice to explain how decision making actually takes place; or, conversely, who believe that what actually occurs somehow sets the standard for what is attainable. In order to avoid this kind of confusion, the first part of the present chapter will concentrate on the question of bureaucratic efficiency, and the later part on explanatory models of bureaucratic functioning; in this way we shall also come to understand their interconnection more clearly.

But why do we need models at all? The reason is that societies are enormously complex, and present formidable problems to those who seek to understand them. The characteristic method of social science is to construct simplified conceptions or models of social life to help define, evaluate or explain this complexity. Of course the world as it is will not exactly match the models we construct. In practice it may be difficult to say whether a particular organization meets the definitional criteria for a bureaucracy; in some respects it may, in others it may not. It will be a matter of degree. In practice we may find that the general principles of organizational efficiency need modification to take account of actual variations in organizational purpose and context. And an explanatory model may require considerable elaboration in order to accommodate the complexity of social reality. But we can only grasp the complexity at all by starting with simplification, and by representing the complexity as so many variations around, or modifications of, or deviations from, the simplification we have constructed. Naturally, if the deviations become too great, we shall need to revise or even abandon our model. In this way the world of actual practice imposes its own discipline upon the flights of intellectual speculation, and provides the decisive test of more or less useful model-building. But to abandon model-building itself is to become bogged down in a morass of descriptive detail, or in interminable lists of principles to meet every possible contingency, such as clog up much of the writing on organization theory.

In this chapter, then, we shall explore the models of bureaucracy developed within the academic disciplines of sociology, political economy and public administration respectively. In doing so we shall find that they differ, not only in terms of their particular focus of interest (social, economic or political), but also in terms of their distinctive method of simplification or model construction. The aim will be to clarify these differences, and to assess whether they are mutually conflicting or complementary; whether, that is to say, they embody antithetical approaches, between which we have to choose, or whether they can be integrated into a larger and more comprehensive theory of bureaucracy.

Bureaucracy and administrative efficiency

The sociology of organization

What do the Vatican and General Motors, NASA and the British Health Service have in common? Organizational sociology sets itself the task of answering such questions, through an exploration of the most general features common to organizations in all sectors of modern society, and by theorizing about the conditions for organizational efficiency, regardless of whether the institution concerned is public or private, sacred or secular, devoted to profits or to preaching, to saving life or to ending it. In doing so it takes its starting point from the work of Max Weber, who was among the first to develop a generalizable theory of organization applicable across modern society. Weber's answer to the above question would have been simple: they are all bureaucracies.

In his definition of bureaucracy, Weber sought to identify the most basic features common to modern systems of large-scale administration. He distinguished ten or eleven of these, but they can be reduced for convenience to four main features. Bureaucratic administration, according to Weber, is characterized by: hierarchy (each official has a clearly defined competence within a hierarchical division of labour, and is answerable for its performance to a superior); continuity (the office constitutes a full-time salaried occupation, with a career structure that offers the prospect of regular advancement); impersonality (the work is conducted according to prescribed rules, without arbitrariness or favouritism, and a written record is kept of each transaction); expertise (officials are selected according to merit, are trained for their function, and control access to the knowledge stored in the files). Together these features constitute Weber's definitional model of bureaucracy: the criteria that a system of administration has to meet for it to be properly called bureaucratic.

But what exactly is administration or a system of administration? At its simplest, administration can be understood as the coordination and execution of policy, and a system of administration as an arrangement of offices concerned with translating policy into directives to be executed at the front line of an organization (shop floor, coal face, battlefield, etc.). That is to say, not everyone who works in a bureaucratic organization is a bureaucrat. As administrators, bureaucrats have to be distinguished from chiefs above, and front-line workers below. Let us consider each of these in turn.

In his discussion of bureaucracy, Weber drew a sharp distinction between an administrative staff and the association or corporate group which employs it. A corporate group is a voluntary or compulsory association of people (anything from a nation down to a trade union, company, political party, university, etc.) which either directly or indirectly elects a leadership or governing body to manage its affairs (cabinet, committee, board, council, etc.). The governing body in turn employs an administrative staff to carry out its policies. This administrative staff, if constituted according to the criteria listed above, will be called a bureaucracy. It is important, therefore, to distinguish between a bureaucracy and the governing body which employs it. The members of each differ crucially in the nature of their position, function and responsibility. Members of a governing body are typically elected and may work only part-time; their function is the broadest formulation of policy and rules for the association, and the provision of the necessary funds for its administration; their responsibility is outwards to the association as a whole (electorate, shareholders, members, etc.). Members of a bureaucracy, in contrast, are always appointed from above, and are responsible to the governing body for the execution of its policy and the administration of its funds. Although this distinction may sometimes be blurred in practice, it is vital in principle.

If at the upper end of an organization the distinction between bureaucrats and chiefs or leaders is relatively clear, drawing a sharp boundary at the lower end is more problematic. According to Weber, the essential characteristic of a bureaucrat is the exercise of authority within a bureau. Production workers neither exercise authority nor work in a bureau. Secretaries or typists are employed in a bureau, and their work is essential to the basic bureaucratic activity of maintaining the files. But they do not exercise authority; they are office workers, not officials. On the other hand, many staff working in government offices at the bottom of its employment hierarchy exercise authority over a relevant public if not over other workers (social security officials, customs officers, etc.). To exclude such archetypically bureaucratic figures from the ranks of a bureaucracy would be paradoxical indeed. So the boundary line cannot simply be drawn above 'front-line workers', as I suggested initially. It depends on the nature of the organization. In a private industry, bureaucratic authority will be coterminous with management; in a government agency, it may extend right down to those who staff the counter, and who comprise an essential part of the administration of policy and the exercise of authority.

Boundaries constitute a problem for any concept, and insistence on precision in all circumstances can become mere pedantry. Provided we are clear that bureaucrats are by definition both subject to higher authority and involved in exercising authority themselves, then we can call those organizations bureaucratic whose administration is arranged according to the principles of Weber's model, even though not everyone working within them, either at the top or bottom of the hierarchy, is necessarily to be counted a bureaucrat.

So far we have been concerned with Weber's definitional model of bureaucracy, with the criteria a system of administration must meet if it is to count as bureaucratic. Many organizational sociologists have accepted Weber's definition because it is clear, precise and generalizable. But Weber also claimed, much more controversially, that the closer an organization approximated to his model, the more efficient it was likely to be; and that it was the superior efficiency of bureaucratic administration that accounted for its general expansion within modern society. In other words, Weber believed that the defining characteristics of bureaucracy were *also* necessary conditions for administrative or organizational efficiency; in effect, that his definitional model served as a normative model as well. 'Experience tends to show,' he wrote, 'that the purely bureaucratic type of administrative organization is, from a purely technical point of view, capable of attaining the highest degree of efficiency . . . it is superior to any other form in precision, in stability, in the stringency of its discipline, and in its reliability'. And in another passage he wrote: 'the fully developed bureaucratic mechanism compares with other organizations exactly as does the machine with the non-mechanical modes of production.'[1]

How did Weber justify this claim? There are two things to note about it at the outset. First, when he insisted on the superiority of bureaucracy, his standard of comparison was not some absolute ideal, but the forms of administration known to past history: by unpaid volunteers, local notables, collegial bodies or kinship networks. To adapt Weber's own analogy, the internal combustion engine may appear wasteful when compared with some ideal of maximum energy utilization, but it is vastly superior to a horse. Secondly, by efficiency Weber meant not one single characteristic, but a complex of values which included quality of performance (e.g. speed, predictability), expansion of scope and cost-effectiveness of operation. These were in his view the characteristics required of an administrative system which had to meet the complex and large-scale administrative needs of a mass industrial society, rather than those of a localized economy geared to the rhythms of nature and the political requirements of a narrow élite.

If we examine the different elements of Weber's bureaucratic model, we can see how each could contribute to meeting these criteria of efficiency. The central feature of bureaucracy is the systematic division of labour, whereby complex administrative problems are broken down into manageable and repetitive tasks, each the province of a particular office, and then coordinated under a centralized hierarchy of command. The mechanical analogy is here quite precise; the subdivision of a complex set of movements into their constituent elements, and their reassembly into a co-ordinated process, achieves an enormous expansion of scope, precision and cost-effectiveness of operation. Other aspects of bureaucracy contribute to the same end. Its impersonality ensures that there is no favouritism either in the selection of personnel, who are appointed according to merit, or in administrative action, which is kept free from the unpredictability of personal connections. Its rule governed character enables a bureaucracy to deal with large numbers of cases in a uniform manner, by means of categorization, while systematic procedures for changing the rules free the administration from the inflexibility of tradition ('the way things have always been done'). For Weber, the contrast with traditional forms of administration offered not only an essential point of comparison, but a means of identifying features of bureaucracy that would otherwise be taken for granted. Thus the separation of the official from ownership of the means of administration ensured that the operation as a whole was freed from the financial limitations of the private household, and that the individual was rendered dependent upon the organization for his or her livelihood, and thus amenable to its discipline. Such factors secured an enormous expansion in administrative capacity and predictability in comparison with the non-bureaucratic systems of the past.

Weber's claim that the defining criteria of bureaucracy also constitute a model of administrative efficiency is one that has been widely challenged by subsequent sociologists. Their studies of how organizations actually work in practice suggest that adherence to bureaucratic norms can hamper efficiency as much as promote it. This is because the principles of bureaucratic organization, so they argue, are more ambiguous than Weber realized, producing significant dysfunctional effects, which become more accentuated the more rigorously the principles are applied. Each, that is to say, has its distinctively pathological manifestation. Adherence to rules can become inflexibility and red tape. Impersonality produces bureaucratic indifference and insensitivity. Hierarchy discourages individual responsibility and initiative. Officialdom in general promotes officiousness, 'officialese' and similar pathologies. Max Weber, it is argued, failed to recognize the ambivalent character of bureaucracy, partly because studies of organization were in their infancy in the early decades of the century. But it was also because his ideas were unduly influenced by the examples of the Prussian army and the Taylorian system of scientific management. The model of machine-like discipline that they both offered obscured key dimensions of organizations, an understanding of which is necessary to secure their efficient operation.

What are these dimensions? They can best be grasped by counterposing to Weber's essentially mechanistic model alternative conceptions of organization developed by later sociologists. One alternative is the idea of an organization as a social system or network of interpersonal relations. Weber's model of organizational efficiency assumes that all aspects of the individual personality which are not relevant to the strict performance of his or her duties will be cast off as they enter the organization, or suppressed through effective socialization. If this were so, then a complete

account of an organization could be given by providing a formal
definition of the duties of each office, and of the relation between
them; efficiency, in turn, would be a matter of securing a rational
division of tasks at every level. In practice, however, people's
personalities are never so totally subsumed into their roles. They
come to the organization as individuals, with personal needs and
expectations for which they seek satisfaction: from social inter-
course at the workplace; from the exercise of skill and a measure of
control over the work process; from being treated 'as people' rather
than as the impersonal occupants of a role. And the manner of their
social interaction at work can be crucial to the effectiveness of their
performance. Any authority which ignores these factors or tries to
suppress them is likely to meet with resistance. People can be
compelled to work upon command, but not to work efficiently or
with commitment. That requires their active cooperation, which
is as much a matter of informal negotiation as of authoritative
command.

A different perspective on organizations is to see them as
communication systems, in which the efficient transmission and
processing of information is necessary to effective decision-taking.
Arguably, Weber's concept of administration put too much emphasis on the execution of policy, to the exclusion of policy
formation and review, both of which require effective mechanisms
for collecting and processing information within the organization.
There are good reasons for believing that a strictly hierarchical
structure is not the most appropriate for these tasks. One is that its
direction of emphasis is from the top downwards, whereas the
transmission of information also requires effective channels of
communication upwards from the grass roots of the organization.
Admittedly, it is always possible for those at the top of a hierarchy
to construct separate institutional arrangements for monitoring
performance outside the normal structures of policy execution. But
this produces wasteful duplication, and in any case those who know
most about the adequacy of a policy are those responsible for
actually administering it. A further defect of hierarchies is that they
are constructed in a pyramidal fashion, narrowing as they approach
the summit. Again, while this may be an effective structure for
sub-dividing tasks and processing instructions downwards, it
creates potentially enormous problems of overload or blockage in
processing information in the opposite direction. Hierarchical

systems suffer from too much information as much as from too little; or, rather, it is information in the wrong place, and it requires sophisticated procedures for sifting as well as transmitting it, if it is to be useful to policy formation and review. This is the argument for decentralized types of organization, in which the responsibility for decision making is pushed downwards to the point where the information is available to make them.

A similar conclusion can be reached from a different conception of organizations, which emphasizes the role of specialist expertise within them. Such a conception typically draws a contrast between two forms of authority,. which, it is argued, Weber did not adequately distinguish. The first is bureaucratic authority, which derives from the occupation of a position or office within a hierarchical structure, and from the powers that reside in the office. The second is the authority which derives from expertise, which resides in the individual as an authority, not in the position he or she occupies. Now Weber would no doubt have said that the two tend to coincide, and that the occupants of a bureaucratic office typically develop their own administrative or managerial expertise. However, this overlooks the fact that most administrators are involved in supervising people with expertise which they do not themselves possess: financial, technical or professional. For these subordinate experts there can be considerable conflict between obedience to the instructions of a superior or the rules of the organization, and obedience to the requirements or principles of their profession. The one involves an externally imposed discipline, the other one that is internal to the nature of the specialism itself. The conclusion is then drawn that the most effective form of organization for experts is not a bureaucratic hierarchy, but a lateral network, whose discipline is maintained by loyalty to the organization as a whole, rather than to the narrowly defined duties of a specific office.

Each of these three alternative conceptions corresponds to a different historical phase in the study of organizations since Weber's time: to a shift from the scientific management to the human relations school; from mechanical to cybernetic or information models; from organizations as hierarchies to organizations as associations of experts. Each has its corresponding prescriptions for organizational efficiency. It follows from the Weberian conception of bureaucracy as a hierarchy of offices that efficiency is to be attained by a rational division of labour, and a clear definition of competences. For those who see organizations as a system of interpersonal relations, efficiency becomes a matter of motivating subordinates within arrangements involving mutual give and take. For those to whom organizations are a communications system, efficiency is to be achieved by the effective sifting and transmission of information, and by locating decisions where such information is most readily available. For those, finally, to whom organization is a matter of the effective application of expertise to essentially technical problems, efficiency means finding arrangements under which experts are best able to exercise their distinctively professional capacities.

Each of these conceptions has in its time been presented as the final truth. It would be more plausible, however, to see them, not as mutually exclusive alternatives, either to the Weberian model or to one another, but as each emphasizing an essential aspect of organizational reality, all of which need taking into account and which together necessitate a modification in the strictly bureaucratic conception of organizational efficiency, rather than its outright replacement. Common to them all is the recognition that authority cannot be just a matter of the assertion of official powers vested in a formal hierarchy or a particular position. This is because subordinates possess their own powers, which reside in informal social networks, in the control of information, or in their own expertise. If the characteristic power of superiors is to initiate, the power of subordinates can be used to modify, delay or obstruct those initiatives. It is the ability to harness such powers to serve the goals of the organization rather than merely the convenience of those who possess them, that constitutes the exercise of authority in its widest sense. From a sociological standpoint, success in this is not primarily a matter of individual personality, but of how the organization itself is structured. Too monolithic a hierarchy will produce a mentality of work to rule; too decentralized a structure without corresponding means of monitoring or influencing performance will produce a work to convenience. Each represents a distinctive form of bureaucratic inertia; in extreme circumstances they can occur simultaneously.

The conclusion that organizations are a combination of formal and informal relations, and that they need to balance the competing requirements of authority and initiative, of command and communication, may seem merely platitudinous. Indeed, it is precisely because general conclusions about organizational efficiency have the quality of platitude that many recent sociologists would argue against generalizing about the matter at all, in abstraction from the particular contexts in which organizations have to operate. There is no one best way, they would argue, there are no universally applicable principles of organizational efficiency. This does not mean that anything goes, or that the question can be reduced to hunch or intuition; but that the criteria for effective operation will vary systematically with the purposes, technology and environment of the organization. On this view, it is the task of theory, not to produce a list of abstract generalizations that are true everywhere, but to discover which types of organization are most appropriate to which particular kinds of context. Let us consider some examples of this more typological theorizing, in the light of the discussion so far.

One of the most influential typologies was that developed by Burns and Stalker in their book *The Management of Innovation*, in which they argued that the decisive variable for organizations is the rate of change in their environment. Organizations which face rapid and persistent change in their markets or their technology, and which thus need to innovate continuously, require a different structure from those whose environment is stable and operations routine. Most appropriate for the latter is what they call a mechanistic structure, which is very similar to the Weberian model of bureaucracy: a hierarchical system of authority, with precise definition of roles and a vertical pattern of communication of decisions and instructions. The former, by contrast, require what they call an organic arrangement: a fluid distribution of functions, with wide scope for individual initiative in defining tasks; authority residing in expertise rather than position; knowledge about the organization as a whole and its goals widely disseminated rather than concentrated at the top; lateral patterns of communication of information and advice; individual commitment to professional norms rather than to the duties of a particular office.

It should be evident that this 'organic' arrangement (it would now be called 'post-bureaucratic') embodies a combination of all the features characteristic of the communications and expertise models considered already. As such it has been criticized as offering a recipe for chaos for any organization which adopts it, and perpetual insecurity for the individuals who work within it. After all, one of the advantages of precise role definition within a division of labour is that individuals can concentrate on the task in hand, without continually questioning the scope of their competence, or having to redefine their relationships with others. Burns and Stalker argue, however, that their mechanistic and organic models should be understood as representing the extreme poles of a spectrum, and that in practice most organizations will be situated within the two extremes. If that is so, then we are back with the idea of a mix or balance of elements, such as we have already considered, albeit with one important difference: the nature of the mix, the precise character of the balance, will vary systematically according to the context or environment of the organization, and the rate of change that imposes on it.

Other sociologists have developed this idea further. Joan Wood-ward (*Industrial Organization*) has shown that the rate of variation within an industry's operations is not just a function of changes in its market or its technology, but also derives from the character of its product. A firm turning out individual customized products will require a more flexible organizational structure than one engaged in assembly-line or continuous-process production. Charles Perrow (*Organizational Analysis: A Sociological View*) argues that the pattern of organization may well vary between different parts of the same firm: a research and development unit requires a much more organic or flexible arrangement of tasks than a production department, whose operations are typically more routine. The two cannot readily be combined within a common structure. Perrow also argues that the differentiation of organizational types is not relevant only to the sphere of industrial production. A similar distinction between different products or processes is to be found within the public service sector. An education or penal institution, for example, which seeks to turn out a conformist product according to a set type, will be run much more bureaucratically than one concerned with individual development or rehabilitation. Here the variation will be the result of the institution's own definition of its goals, rather than inherent in the nature of the activity itself.

Two conclusions can be drawn about organizational efficiency from this discussion. The first is that a structure which works effectively in one context may not in another. Bureaucratic pathology is not so much a matter of exaggerated hierarchy or rule following as such, but its inappropriateness to the goals of a particular organization in a given environment. Secondly, efficiency is itself a many-layered concept, whose different elements are not necessarily mutually consistent. An organization whose operations are highly routinized may be very cost-efficient, but for that very reason be incapable of responding quickly to some sudden and unexpected change in the environment. The dinosaurs were very efficient organizations for converting food into predatory muscle-power, but they went out of business. On the other hand, a looser system which is more innovative and responsive to change may be very wasteful of resources. Effectiveness or appropriateness in a given context is a very different matter from simple cost-efficiency.

How far do such conclusions invalidate Weber's model, with which we began? We have seen that most sociologists would accept Weber's definition of bureaucracy, but question his claim that it is necessarily the most efficient form of organization. However, the suggestions made for replacing it with alternative models of organizational structure are not wholly convincing. It is difficult to find many successful examples of an organic administrative model in practice, and those that do exist either subsequently develop in a bureaucratic direction as the organization expands and ages, or else are to be found located as units within a larger bureaucratic whole. The conclusion that the typical modern form of large-scale administrative organization is indeed hierarchical, impersonal, rule-governed, etc., is hard to resist. What is at issue is the *degree* to which these characteristics should be emphasized, and what other aspects of an organization need to be taken into account if we are to understand it adequately. As suggested earlier, it is a matter of modification in, or variations around, Weber's bureaucratic model, rather than its outright replacement. Indeed, the model can perhaps best be regarded as identifying simply the most general structural features of modern administration, rather than as offering a detailed prescription for organizational practice. Like all models, that is to say, it provides a useful starting point, rather than a final resting place, for analysis.

It remains to review what is distinctive about the sociology of organization in its approach to the study of bureaucracy. As its name implies, sociology is concerned with the social in its most general sense, and the sociology of organization with the study of organizational forms across all sectors of social life, regardless of whether they are located in the public or private domain, in the sphere of production or social welfare. Appropriate to this broad focus of interest, as we have seen, is an inclusive rather than exclusive definition of bureaucracy, which serves to identify the most typical features of modern administration in general.

Besides its general focus of interest, however, sociology is also characterized by a distinctive method of analysis, or model-building, as I have called it. Its method is to approach the study of social formations by first identifying their overall structure, the systematic interrelationship of their elements, and to understand the part or the individual in terms of its situation within this totality. So the sociology of organization is concerned to grasp the way bureaucracy is structured, as a systematic relationship of elements, whether these elements are defined as roles within a hierarchical division of labour, as a set of interconnected features (rules, impersonality, specialization, etc.) or as different interacting dimensions of a complex totality (formal and informal systems). Whatever the differences between individual sociologists over the precise definition of these elements, they will agree that organizational efficiency is dependent in the first instance on how the interrelationship between them is structured in practice. Such an approach is at the opposite pole from one which starts with the individual personality or personality-type, and conceives efficiency as a matter of ensuring that the right individual is in the right place at the right time. It is also different from the kind of model-building which constructs a theory of bureaucracy starting from an abstract conception of the individual, defined independently of any time or place. It is to just such a theory that I turn in the next section.

Political economy

As its name implies, political economy approaches the study of bureaucracy from an economic point of view. This means not only that it is concerned with the way organizations are financed, and with the effects the form of financing has upon the way they function. It is also that, in its neo-classical form at least, political economy locates bureaucracies on one side of a fundamental divide between two contrasting methods of social coordination: markets and hierarchies. Markets are arrangements which coordinate the actions of large numbers of people automatically, and on a lateral basis, through the operation of the price mechanism, without infringing their freedom or requiring inequalities of status. Hierarchies, by contrast, coordinate action vertically, via a structure of consciously exercised authority and compulsion, in which people's status is by definition unequal. We shall consider later some of the implications of this distinction. For the present we should note that political economy proceeds to draw a further contrast, between two different types of hierarchy: those which are situated within a market environment (firms) and those which are not (bureaucracies). In contrast to the sociology of organization, political economy embraces an exclusive rather than inclusive definition of bureaucracy: only those types of hierarchy which operate outside a market environment are bureaucratic.

If political economy's focus of interest is different from that of sociology, so too is its characteristic method of analysis, or model-building. Its starting point lies not with the social totality and the way it is structured, but with the individual, as conceived independently of any particular context. From this starting point, the method seeks to explain the different kinds of social institution that exist by demonstrating their necessity to the individuals so conceived. In other words, it asks the question: if individuals are as we assume they are, what social arrangements or institutions would they find necessary? We should note that the method does not pretend to offer a historical account of the origins of such institutions, but rather to explain the form they have come to take, and their continued existence, in terms of their ability to satisfy the purposes of individuals. Of all forms of model-building in the social sciences, this makes the most ambitious claims for its ability to construct a complex social world by strict deduction from the simplest of premises. Starting from these premises, we shall follow the model through until we reach bureaucracy. Those impatient to go straight to our subject should appreciate that it is of the essence of any deductive method that the earlier stages of the argument are essential to the later.

The individuals who constitute the subjects of political economy are conceived as purposive agents, who pursue their own individual interest or advantage in a rational, i.e. calculating, manner. Since such agents are not self-sufficient, they need the assistance of others to achieve their purposes. This assistance is typically sought through relations of exchange. The distinctive characteristic of an exchange relationship, as Adam Smith pointed out, is that one party to it can only obtain what he or she wants through satisfying the wants of another; it is a relationship based upon a mutuality of self-interest. In many spheres of life, such relations are determined personally, on an individual basis, and the precise nature of the bargain struck may never be made explicit (association, friendship, marriage). Where the same exchange is repeated on many occasions by many different people, we can talk of a market, in which the terms of the bargain are determined impersonally and explicitly, according to the relative demand and supply of the goods being exchanged. Markets have many well-known (and much-applauded) characteristics, of which only one will concern us for the moment: they carry with them their own system of rewards and penalties, incentives and sanctions, which are imposed automatically. If you possess some commodity that is valued highly on the market, for whatever reason, you will receive a lot in exchange; if you have nothing that is so valued, or that is insufficiently valued, you will receive little or nothing in return. In extreme cases you may starve. If so, it is a death penalty that is executed, as it were, automatically and impersonally, not by personal decree or conscious human agency.

Not all social life can be carried on according to relations of exchange, nor all economic activity by means of market relations. In modern economies, the market has to be supplemented by two forms of hierarchy: one that is constituted within the market (firms), the other outside it (government or bureaucracy). The necessity for each can be demonstrated from the same premise as that of the market itself: the pursuit of their self-interest by individuals. Let us start with the theory of the firm. If every single operation in a complex process of production were carried out by separate producers, each exchanging their goods and services with one another on the market, the result would be an enormous waste of resources through the necessity of multiple transactions, with their communication and information costs, etc. Market selection would itself ensure that the cost of such transactions was reduced, by the coordination of these operations on non-market principles within a single firm. The spontaneous division of labour coordinated externally by the market would come to be replaced by an internal and consciously arranged coordination of the division of labour by administrative means.

But why should this internal coordination be arranged hierarchically, and not by lateral cooperation between equals? A common sense answer might be that the internal hierarchy of the firm is the product of a pre-existing structure of ownership. However, political economy leaves nothing to common sense, and refuses to take ownership for granted. It identifies the explanation for hierarchy in the problems of maintaining cooperation between self-interested individuals within non-market relations. Where an equal share of the product is guaranteed to all, so it is argued, each has an incentive to secure some additional personal benefit through reduced effort or shirking; and the incentive is the greater, the larger the association, and the less difference one person's effort will make to the overall product. After all, labour is by definition something unpleasant, which we all avoid if we can. So everyone comes to have an interest in the creation of a system of supervision, which will monitor the work of each, and devise a framework of rewards and penalties to secure maximum performance overall. Unlike the incentives and sanctions of the market, which operate 'naturally', this is an artificial construction consciously designed to modify the direction of individual self-interest, so that it works to further the interest of all. But what incentive will the supervisors have in their turn to perform their supervision adequately? Only if at the top of the hierarchy there is an individual or group, whose reward is dependent upon the performance of the firm as a whole in the market, and who gain or lose according to the effectiveness of their coordination and supervision. Here is one characteristic justification for the profit-taking entrepreneur.

If the firm is defined as a hierarchy that operates within the market, and subject to its incentives and sanctions, government bureaucracies are hierarchies which operate outside them. The necessity for government can be readily demonstrated from the same premises considered already. People in pursuit of their individual interest will not only engage in relations of exchange, but will be inclined not to keep their bargains, to take what is not their own, etc. If such behaviour were generalized, exchange could never take place at all. A necessary condition for the market to operate, therefore, is a framework of legal compulsion: to guarantee the security of person and property, the integrity of contracts and the soundness of the monetary system. Such a framework could never itself be supplied on market principles, nor yet by voluntary subscription, and therefore has to be financed through compulsory taxation by government. Beyond the provision of internal order and external defence, governments also have a role in supplying those other public goods which would be provided either sufficiently, or only with great inconvenience, if charged for at the point of provision (roads, education, scientific research, etc.). Although political economists disagree about how far it is necessary or desirable to extend this list, it is clear that all these functions require an extensive hierarchy to administer. Such forms of administrative hierarchy are called 'bureaucracies', because they are financed outside the market.

We have now reached the point where we are able to provide a clear definition of bureaucracy, and to explore why political economy concludes that bureaucracies are inevitably inefficient. One final preliminary point of clarification, however, is needed. In the academic division of labour, the study of markets is defined as the province of neo-classical economics, and the application of its assumptions to the study of hierarchies, especially government hierarchies, as the province of a separate discipline called the theory of public or rational choice. The literature devoted to the public choice approach to politics is now enormous. However, since its basic methodology and assumptions are drawn from economics, and from the study of market behaviour, I have chosen to use the older designation political economy, as more accurately characterizing the relation between the economic and political aspects of the same body of theory.

According to political economy, then, a bureaucracy is an administrative hierarchy which is financed by a grant rather than by the sale of its product on the market. As I indicated in the Introduction to this book, such a grant can be provided either by voluntary subscription, or through compulsory taxation. We are concerned here primarily with the latter, i.e. with government bureaucracies, though it is important to recognize that there are many examples of the former (e.g. churches, political parties), and that they function on similar principles. It should also be noted that not all government activities are financed out of taxation. A state-owned motor manufacturing company, which sells its product in a competitive market, is more like a firm than a bureaucracy. Somewhere in between are the public utilities, which, although they mostly sell their product at a unit price, are 'natural' monopolies and therefore not subject to market competition. They are more like a bureaucracy than a firm. The core of government activities, however, is bureaucratic in the strictest sense.

The point of defining bureaucracy in this way is to indicate that the source and context of financing is crucial to determining the efficiency of an administrative hierarchy. We have seen that the purpose of such a hierarchy is not only to coordinate the internal division of labour, but also to provide supervision against shirking. The ultimate guarantee of the strictness of this supervision within firms is the incentive and sanction of the market; a firm in which shirking is widespread will be taken over or go out of business. Bureaucracies, however, are not subject to the same sanction, because they are not financed through the market. Since they cannot go out of business, there is no pressure on those at the top of the hierarchy to ensure strict supervision, and eliminate feather-bedding. Nor is there any positive incentive for them either, through a share in increased profits. The only way for senior bureaucrats to increase their own benefits substantially is through organizational expansion, rather than organizational efficiency, since their payment, power and prestige are typically related to size. A larger hierarchy also means more strata to coordinate, more memoranda to duplicate and more work for everyone to do, though not necessarily any significant increase in any other measurable output of the organization.

Bureaucracies thus succeed in combining two apparently contradictory failings: chronic shirking on the one hand, and making work on the other. Nor does this exhaust the sorry catalogue. If the bureaucracy is one whose purpose is to serve the public directly, there will be no market pressure to ensure consumer satisfaction; its customers or clients cannot vote with their feet and take their custom elsewhere. In the absence of any such external sanctions or incentives, the tendency will be for a bureaucracy to serve the convenience of those who work within it, rather than the customers for whose benefit it supposedly exists.

Shirking, making work, indifference to the consumer: what are these but the typical subjects of public complaint and popular legend about bureaucracy throughout its history? Admirals without fleets, hospitals without patients, gas fitters without tools: the situations and characters satirized in television programmes such as *Yes, Minister* are simply logical extrapolations from everyday observation about how bureaucracies work. If Weberians are impressed by the efficiency of bureaucracy in comparison with traditional systems of administration, political economists are equally impressed by their inefficiency in comparison with hierarchies which operate within the market. Their point of comparison is wholly different. Nor is that all. They also claim that the inefficiency is one that can be predicted (and hence explained) on the basis of elementary assumptions about how individual behaviour responds to the presence, or absence, of key incentives and sanctions.

This line of argument had a very practical consequence during the 1980s, in providing the justification for successive governments in the English-speaking world to reduce the size of government, to privatize its services, and to subject those that remained to the wholesome disciplines of the market. But does the conclusion about bureaucratic inefficiency follow quite so inexorably from its underlying premise? There are a number of political economists who accept the validity of the starting point and its assumptions about human nature, but who question whether such a sharp contrast can be sustained between bureaucracies and firms. From one side the argument seeks to show that bureaucracies operate under competitive pressures of their own which discourage inefficiency. Government bureaucracy is not a single monolith, but comprises separate departments, all competing against each other for scarce Treasury funds. The wasteful are unlikely to be rewarded with success in such competition. And what incentive do the Treasury itself and its political masters have to exercise its supervision effectively? One answer is that the politicians operate in an electoral marketplace, and face the threat of 'takeover' by a rival political party, promising the electorate to 'cut out waste' if they themselves do not.

However, the analogy is not an exact one, because of the difficulty of telling whether bureaucratic provision is wasteful or not. It is a cardinal point of political economy that the prime test of efficient operation is provided by the price indicators of the competitive market. Where government services cannot be assessed against this test, e.g. by putting them out to competitive tender, there is no way of telling whether or when they are being efficiently provided. Politicians thus face a characteristic dilemma. A right wing strategy of cutting budgets to eliminate waste usually ends up by cutting services as well. And electorates are just as keen to preserve or expand services as they are to eliminate waste. On the other hand, a left wing strategy for public sector expansion can provide a field day for bureaucratic 'make-work' and 'feather-bedding', and this can prove equally unpopular, especially when exposed to the negative reaction of the international financial markets. Each strategy meets its distinctive electoral reckoning. The theory of bureaucracy thus has its own contribution to make to explaining the swings and roundabouts of electoral politics.

If one group of objectors to the sharp distinction drawn between firms and bureaucracies thus seeks to argue, not altogether successfully, that bureaucracies are like firms because they operate in an electoral market-place, another argues that firms are really more like bureaucracies. Or, to put the point more precisely, the modern business corporation has features which make it as much like a bureaucracy as the firm of neo-classical theory. This is so in two respects. First, with the separation of ownership from control in the modern corporation, the senior executives who effectively determine its policies occupy salaried positions, just like the bureaucrat. Even where they enjoy share options, it is the salary that is their chief source of income and that determines their behaviour. And since salary levels are related to the size of the organization and its turnover, they share the same interest as government bureaucrats in the growth and expansion of their organizations.

It can be contended, or course, that, in contrast to government bureaucracies, the growth of business corporations is economically self-sustaining, and depends upon maintaining profitability. But there are reasons for believing that size also encourages in-efficiency. Beyond a certain point, economies of scale are offset by the increasing cost of internal communication and control. At the same time increasing size enables the corporation to manipulate the market, through strategies of price fixing, discouraging new entrants, etc. Here is a second point of similarity between corporations and bureaucracies. Markets in real life are never as perfect as the theories suppose. Imperfect competition is still competition, but it reduces some of the presumed advantages that firms enjoy over bureaucracies in respect of the pressures making for efficiency.

The antithesis between firms and bureaucracies thus turns out to be an ideal-typical one; that is to say, the two types represent two ends of a spectrum of possibilities. Business corporations in the actual world share some of the characteristics of firms and some of bureaucracies. It is because they do so that recent theorizing in the public choice school has sought to develop a general theory of bureaucracy applicable to governments and business corporations alike. One problem that is common to bureaucratic hierarchies, it is argued, whatever the relative degree of their *incentive* to ensure strict supervision over subordinates, is the extent of their *capacity* to do so. If salaried staff once appointed can only be dismissed for fraud or substantial incompetence, then within these limits self-interested individuals will act in ways which promote their own advantage rather than the goals of the organization, wherever the two diverge. Formal authority is inadequate to cope with this problem of organizational slack or slippage. It can only be overcome by a bargaining process, in which all kinds of informal benefits or perks are exchanged in return for particular levels of performance. At this point the difference between government and business re-emerges as a difference in the respective range and value of the perks available to each in this bargaining process, which enables the latter to secure the motivation of its subordinates more effectively than the former. Business simply has more perks to offer.

It is significant that even attempts within the assumptions of political economy to develop a general theory of administration applicable to both government and business corporations should end up demonstrating the superior efficiency of the latter. As we have seen, this is the whole tendency of its approach throughout, despite some qualifications. Its conclusions about the inefficiency of government bureaucracy derive from two basic assumptions. The first is that the key to efficiency lies in the incentives and sanctions of the competitive market. Whatever imperfections may exist in actual markets are not to be compared with removal from the discipline of the market altogether. It is this removal that distinguishes bureaucracy as a different species of administrative hierarchy from the firm. This conclusion is underpinned by a second assumption, about the self-interested character of human dispositions. People are only brought to work for the goals of an organization by means of incentives and sanctions which align the individual interest with the general one. In the absence of such incentives and sanctions, or of supervisors with an interest in applying them effectively, individuals will shirk or do their own thing. This is the potential dilemma of all hierarchies, but one that is actualized in a bureaucracy.

Deductive theories are only as good as the assumptions on which they are based. The assumption of political economy about the self-interested disposition of human nature is obviously a narrow one. This is both an advantage and a disadvantage. The advantage is its capacity to provide a powerful explanatory tool from the simplest of starting points. But the tool becomes less useful to the extent that other more complex dispositions come into play. Attempts to incorporate these within the ambit of the model by extending the concept of self-interest to include any end the agent chooses to pursue (including the interests of others), are self-defeating, because they deprive the model of the predictive power which is its chief strength. This problem may not be acute in the domain of economic activity, which is characterized by the pursuit of private advantage anyway. But it becomes so as one moves outside this sphere. It is precisely the relevance of assumptions drawn from an economic context to the understanding of government, and its bureaucracy, that is questioned by the discipline of public administration, which we turn to next.

Public administration

Some students of public administration would dispute whether there is any single distinctive body of theory or standpoint which characterizes their discipline, or even whether there is any principled difference between management in the public and private spheres. Indeed, as government itself becomes increasingly market-oriented, and subject to private-sector techniques of organization, so the political economy or public choice approach already considered would seem increasingly appropriate to its analysis. The limitations of this approach, however, can best be understood by counterposing to it an older tradition of analysis, whose significance becomes evident as the practical limitations of treating government as a defective form of market institution are themselves exposed to view. To call this tradition of analysis that of public administration *tout court* may be an oversimplification; but it is one which helps highlight a contrasting standpoint and methodology to that of political economy.

Let us start with the concept of the public itself. As we have seen, political economy's approach to the public sphere is a largely negative one. It defines the market as conceptually prior to government, with the latter comprising a residual category of functions that the market is unable to perform. Besides being conceptually prior, the market is also seen as preferable in principle as a method of social coordination, since it involves transactions that are voluntary, lateral and decentralized, in contrast to the compulsory, hierarchical and centralized activities of government. Such an antithesis readily generates the conclusion that the public sphere should be confined to the absolutely necessary minimum of market-supporting functions.

The study of public administration offers an altogether different conception of the public sphere, in which the idea of the public is given central emphasis. This concept has a number of different meanings. First is the idea of the public as that which touches all citizens, and the arrangements of society as a whole, in potentially any aspect. Anything may become a legitimate object of public action, if it concerns all, or fulfils a recognized social need. And since individuals are many-sided, and social life is complex, the tasks of public administration will be correspondingly varied. They cannot be reduced to a mere appendage of the economy. Secondly, the public connotes not only that which is of general concern, but that which is carried on in public, subject to public view. Of course the extent to which this is so will be different between different political systems, and a matter of dispute within them; but the principle that that which is carried on in the name of all should be subject to public inspection and public accountability is a cardinal point of difference from administration within a private organization or enterprise. Thirdly, the concept of the public suggests a form of administration which is carried out for the public, according to a norm or ethos of public service. The designation of the administrator as a civil or public servant, rather than as a manager, may contain an element of idealization, but the term itself indicates something of the expectations held about the way in which the function will be carried out. These different dimensions of the public constitute cumulative points of contrast with private business, and call into question the extent to which conceptions of efficiency or models of organization and human behaviour derived from the one can be applied without qualification to the other.

Take for example the definition of efficiency. We have already noted an important distinction between the effectiveness of a service, and the cost-efficiency of its provision. But what counts as an effective service in the context of government? The product of government is not specific and readily measurable, like the output of a firm, but general and diffuse. Consider such diverse agencies as a health authority, a police force and an army. What exactly is their product, effective delivery of which constitutes an index of their efficiency? Health, law-enforcement and national security would be the obvious answers. But are these to be measured by the diseases, crimes and wars successfully *prevented*, or those successfully cured, solved and fought once they have broken out?

Prevention of an evil is presumably better than its cure. But successful prevention is difficult to measure, depending as it does upon counterfactual claims; and in any case it requires the coordination of policy between many different departments. It follows that the demand for a quantitative index of output and hence of effectiveness from the separate agencies of government will itself skew their efforts towards cure rather than prevention, because it is something measurable and under their own control. A health service can more readily measure the effectiveness of its contribution to curing lung cancer than to preventing it, a police force its contribution to solving violent crime than to reducing its incidence, since both are the product of factors outside the agency's own control. If we are seriously concerned about prevention, then effectiveness becomes much more a matter of the coordination of policy across different departments or agencies, than the measurement of output from any one.

Decisions about how to define or measure effectiveness are thus themselves qualitative or political judgements. The same goes for judgements about what level of service is sufficient to constitute an effective provision. Up to what point should life be preserved, road safety be secured, or education be provided? At what level should provision be made for the unemployed, the handicapped or the immobile? It can be argued that qualitative decisions of this kind are made in private industry every day in judgements about how to balance the quality of a product against the cost of its production. But the 'correctness' of such decisions is validated by the quantitative index of the profit level, and is ultimately therefore a technical judgement about what the market will bear. In the non-market sector, where supply is related to need rather than to effective demand, such judgements are irreducibly qualitative. Whose need is to be met: that of society or the individual? How are such needs to be defined? Up to what cost should they be satisfied? These are political judgements. And since in practice judgements about the cost-efficiency of a given service cannot be divorced from questions about the level of its provision, those too become political. Criteria set nationally for the unit cost of a hospital bed, for example, a pupil place, or a passenger transport mile, are as much targets for the level of service to be provided as they are indices for the cost-efficiency of its provision.

A distinguishing feature of public administration, then, is the political character of its services. The content and level of such services is determined by qualitative judgements, and by a publicly defensible compromise between competing values, rather than by any single criterion such as profitability. The demand to meet business criteria of efficiency is itself a political demand which has consequences for the nature and level of the service provided. Public administration is thus not a matter of carrying out goals set by the politician in the most cost-efficient manner. It is a matter of administering policy in accordance with the values which have determined it, among which considerations of cost-efficiency may have a smaller or a larger place. Ends and means interconnect, in other words; policy and its administration are not rigidly separable.

A clear example of this interconnection is the general requirement of public administration to treat like cases alike, and to operate in a strictly rule-governed and impersonal manner. This is not an instrumental requirement to maximize efficiency of output, but a substantive value embodying ideas about the rule of law and equality of citizenship rights. A businessman who bends the rules is showing flexibility, and a rule book which is highly general allows scope for individual initiative in the pursuit of profit. A civil servant who does the same is guilty of misconduct, and a rule book which allows large discretion to the official in dealings with the public is inviting arbitrariness in the treatment of different citizens. Rule keeping is not a means to the end of profit, to be varied if the occasion demands, but a value in itself. It is for this reason that the Weberian model of bureaucracy, with its emphasis on the principle of legal rationality, is particularly appropriate to the public sphere. Public administration, in fact, is a combination of two competing practices, law and management: the effective delivery of a product, and the interpretation and application of legal rules. The precise balance between the two will differ according to the nature of the service (policing, welfare provision, water supply). But tensions between the two practices are not always easy to reconcile, and they constitute a typical source of those charges of red tape, to which public administration is characteristically more prone than private industry.

Public administration thus differs crucially from private business in the nature of its activity, as providing for the most general public needs, and in a manner that meets both political and legal criteria of performance. It also differs in the form of discipline to which it is subject. Here the second concept of the public mentioned above comes into play: the public as publicity. The standard of performance of private business, as we have seen, is regulated by market competition and the rate of profit. Preoccupied as it is with the wholesome influence of these disciplines, political economy notices only their absence in the public sector, rather than the presence of a distinctive discipline of its own: that of public scrutiny. Government administration is subject to a whole variety of levels and kinds of scrutiny, which typically include: a general accountability of the executive to a parliament for the conduct of its business, both directly and via independent audit commissions; the investigation of individual areas of administration by specialist committees; the recourse of the citizen to elected representatives, to an Ombudsman, or to the courts, in the event of maladministration. What is at issue in such scrutiny is not merely the cost-efficiency of public provision, but whether money is spent for the purpose and on the terms for which it was voted, and administration conducted in accordance with legally defined powers, and the legally established rights of the citizen.

To say that public administration is subject to public scrutiny is not to say that it is necessarily carried out in the constant glare of publicity. Much administration could not be so carried on, and in addition government bureaucracy has its own pressures to secretiveness and monopolization of information which threaten the effectiveness of scrutiny procedures in the same way as the monopolistic tendencies of corporations threaten the effectiveness of market discipline. The conflict between bureaucratic secretiveness and the openness required by the principle of public accountability is one to which I shall return in a later chapter. But what this principle requires is, first, that there be routine forms of accountability to which administration is subject; and, secondly, the possibility that any decision may *become* public if it touches a matter of sufficient public interest. A routine decision to allow a planning application for a new building or a change of land use; to subsidize a particular artistic production; to release a prisoner on parole: any of these may go public because they touch on fundamental issues of policy or value controversy. And if they do, it will not only be the content of the decision, but the manner in which it has been taken that will be under inspection. So it is not that public administration is subject to constant public gaze, but the knowledge that at any point it might become so, that forms part of the discipline of its accountability.

There is a final aspect of the definition of the public which makes its own contribution to the performance of government administration, and that is the existence of a public service ethos: certain beliefs and norms of conduct that are inseparable from the role and privileges of the civil servant. These include features such as a concern for the public interest in preference to private or sectional ones; a belief in the value of the collective provision of essential services; a due regard for the law and legally established rights, as well as for the conscientious performance of the duties of office. The chronic dilemma of bureaucratic inefficiency, which political economists attribute to government, is in part the product of their extending the self-interest assumption to the point where the goal of any administrator becomes to do anything *except* promote the aims of the organization in a conscientious manner, unless there is a specific inducement to do so. That is to push the assumption to the point of absurdity. Of course there are incentives and sanctions associated with a public service ethos, as there are with any normative order; accelerated or retarded promotion is only the most obvious of these. But to see administrative behaviour as subject to a constant calculation of self-interest is to overlook what is distinctive about social norms of conduct: whether by a process of conscious acceptance or unconscious internalization, they become recognized as valid or binding on the individual, and hence an autonomous determinant of action.

It is doubtful, in fact, whether a coherent account even of economic activity can be given from a rigorous assumption of self-interest alone. The fundamental distinction that political economy seeks to make between hierarchical and market relations cannot be sustained simply in terms of an unequal distribution of resources, which enables superiors to control subordinates, since such a phenomenon typifies exchange relations as well as hierarchies. The concept of a hierarchy is only distinguishable in terms of authority positions that are recognized as legitimate, and rules of conduct that are recognized as binding: i.e. by the presence of a normative order defining the relations between superiors and subordinates. Once this is acknowledged, then there is nothing surprising in the conclusion that different hierarchies have their own norms of conduct; and that, if the distinctive ethos of the business corporation is the pursuit of private advantage, that of public administration is more directed towards norms of public service. Indeed, by a process of further differentiation, it is possible to identify a characteristic ethos which distinguishes different government departments or agencies, and which is the product of a tradition of experience in dealing with particular types of problem. It is often pointed out, for example, that the British Home Office, with its primarily regulatory functions and mentality, has never provided a particularly sympathetic environment for such concerns as children's welfare, civil liberties, or racial policy, because these run counter to its dominant outlook.

What have such considerations to do with efficiency? The general conclusion to which they lead is that any discussion of efficiency cannot be divorced from an understanding of the distinctive activity or practice of the institution under examination. As we have seen, even the definition of what counts as efficiency or effectiveness depends upon the nature and purposes of the activity in which it is engaged. The purposes of government are many and interconnected, and the criteria for assessing the effectiveness of its administration are correspondingly varied as well as politically contested. But however these come to be defined, government administration has its own norms and procedures for securing effective performance, which are integral to its distinctive activity: a public service ethos, and a discipline of public accountability. And within these general features, different departments or agencies will have their own distinctive philosophy, sensitivity to which is necessary to ensuring efficient practice. To understand the full significance of the public in public administration, therefore, is to understand both the criteria and conditions for its effective operation, and its difference from private business. While certain of the latter's techniques may have their place in the public arena, to transpose its procedures wholesale is to ignore this basic distinction. It is a distinction which the definition of bureaucracy as public administration serves to underline.

It should by now be clear what is the distinctive approach adopted within the study of public administration to its subject matter. Most students of public administration would no doubt reject the suggestion that they are engaged in anything as grandiose as model-building; their work is largely descriptive and historical in its method. However, such an approach or method itself implies a particular theory of social and political institutions. This is that to explain what happens within them, we need to understand their distinctive character or ethos, the nature of the activity in which they are engaged, and the values implicit in this activity. Administrative methods or arrangements which are consistent with this ethos are likely to prove effective; those that run counter to it will not. In other words, attention to the culture of an organization, and its distinctive form of practice, provides the key to its understanding.

This approach explains the importance of comparative analysis to the study of public administration, since it is only through comparison that the distinctiveness of an organization's culture can be identified, and that it can be seen as a social product rather than the result of human nature. So far we have been mainly concerned with exploring the contrast between business and public administration, in order to elucidate the distinctiveness of the latter. But if we make the comparison between different countries, we shall find that the degree to which that contrast is marked will differ between them. In the USA, the ethos of government administration is closer to business than it is in Britain or France, where the civil service constitutes a more closed and exclusive élite. (For this reason it is perhaps not surprising that the USA should be the main source of attempts to extend rational choice assumptions from the economic to the political sphere.) Yet if a public service ethos is less developed in the USA, this is compensated for by a much more stringent requirement of openness in government, and a much more rigorous investigative process – both based upon a more thorough constitutional separation of powers, and a culture altogether less deferential than in either Britain or France. In other words, the respective part played by a public service ethos and procedures of public accountability in securing efficient administration will vary between different countries.

Such differences, however, appear less marked if we extend the range of comparison to political systems beyond the established liberal democracies. The significance of dictatorships, in this context, is that they are by definition subject to little public accountability, whether through political institutions to a public opinion, or through legal ones to the rule of law. They therefore constitute a useful test of the value of the public domain to administrative efficiency. Many believe that the rule of a strong figure, whatever its disadvantages, will at least be efficient, since its administrators will be subject to decisive political direction, and to harsh sanctions for inadequate performance. But such a belief has less to do with reality than with the self-image of dictators themselves, who typically justify their power on the grounds that they have displaced the ineffectual talking shops of parliament, and made the trains run on time. Contemporary research to expose such pretensions is by definition difficult, if not hazardous. But historical research reveals these in reality to be highly personalized regimes, whose administration is subject to the shifting require-ments of maintaining the dictator's position, which is inherently insecure. Lacking legitimacy, dictators will tend to develop compet-ing administrative agencies, which can be played off against each other; to make appointments on grounds of loyalty rather than ability; and to treat government administration as the basis for personal reward rather than public service. The typical result is chronic coordination problems, low quality of administrative cadres, and the exploitation of public office for private gain. The rational choice conception of bureaucracy as a system of adminis-tration whose members seek to maximize their personal advantage without any external discipline does indeed exist; but it is a pathological phenomenon, typical of dictatorships, where the open accountability of a properly 'public' administration is lacking.

A different set of questions is raised by the contrast between the character of public administration in developed economies and some developing ones: in particular, whether a bureaucratic system can operate effectively in the context of a culture that provides only weak support to some of its essential features. On the one hand there is the disjunction between the characteristically bureaucratic requirements of appointment by merit, impersonality and rule-governed procedure, and the relationships of a traditional society determined according to status, kinship or ethnicity. On the other hand the dominant position of government administration within an economy which may provide relatively few other employment

opportunities, and within a polity whose other political institutions
may be only weakly developed, makes it difficult to subject it to any
systematic discipline. Admittedly it is not easy to isolate the purely
administrative element in government performance from the sheer
difficulty of the tasks of economic development and nation-building
pursued under unfavourable circumstances. Yet these tasks and
circumstances themselves affect the character of the administrative
system. Divorced from, yet also penetrated by, the traditional
society which it seeks to transform, government administration is
typically subject to the pull of conflicting cultural norms and
expectations.

In conclusion, it can be argued that comparative analysis not only
reveals the variety and distinctiveness of organizational cultures –
attention to which is relevant to their quality of performance – it
also underlines the conditions needed to sustain an effective system
of public administration. For different reasons, dictatorial regimes
and many developing countries possess only a weak public service
ethos and procedures of public accountability. Their adminis-
trations are often criticized for bureaucratic arbitrariness or ar-
rogance. It may be questioned, however, how far the designation
bureaucratic is appropriate at all, if they deviate systematically from
the strictly Weberian criteria of bureaucracy: rule-governed procedure, and the impersonal treatment of cases 'without passion or
bias'. Such criteria require both a tradition of the rule of law, and an
attentive public to sustain.

Overview

The purpose of this survey of how bureaucracy is treated within the
three disciplines has been to clarify the differences in their
definition of the concept, and in their respective approaches to the
question of administrative efficiency. It has also sought to identify
the reasons for these differences, in their differing conceptions of
method, and divergent focus of interest. Should we then conclude
from such a survey that there can be no agreement on how
bureaucracy is to be defined, or on the criteria and conditions for
administrative efficiency? Is it all simply a question of our initial
standpoint or disciplinary perspective? Before we hasten to draw
such a conclusion, we ought first to explore whether there is any
common ground between the respective approaches, or any way of

integrating them within the framework of a more general theory of bureaucracy. In doing this we shall naturally have to move beyond the confines of any one disciplinary position.

Let us take the definitional question first. As we have seen, the sociology of organization adopts an inclusive concept of bureaucracy, since its interest lies in modern organizations as a whole, and its concern is with their most general features (though it also recognizes differences between them). For political economy and public administration, on the other hand, it is the differences that are the most significant, whether in their method of funding, or mode of accountability; and they therefore adopt an exclusive definition of bureaucracy which limits it to grant-funded organizations or public administration respectively. If we stand outside the particular disciplines, however, there is no reason why we should give priority either to what organizations have in common, or to what differentiates them. Both are important to a general theory of bureaucracy, and we therefore need a conceptual strategy that will encompass both. The most obvious strategy is to use the term bureaucracy in the wider Weberian sense of those criteria typical of modern large-scale administration in general, and then to identify the most important lines of variation or differentiation within this wider category. We need, that is to say, both a conception of bureaucracy in general, and a typology of bureaucracies; we shall need to talk both of bureaucracy as such, and of particular bureaucratic *types*.

Which, then, are the most significant lines of differentiation that will give us a coherent typology of bureaucracies? According to the sociology of organization, the key variable is organizational structure: this will be more rigid or more flexible, with more or less detailed role definition and control over front-line workers, according to the organization's goal or product, and the environment in which it operates. For political economy, the most important differentiating feature is the method by which an organization is financed: whether from a grant or by the unit sale of its product. For public administration, the key variable is the manner of an organization's accountability, whether public or private. We thus have three distinct principles of differentiation (see the diagram, p. 40).

The only good reason for assigning any one of the three dimensions exclusive priority would be if it could be shown to be the

Dimensions of bureaucratic differentiation

Character of goal or product	Rigid organizational structure	Flexible structure
Method of financing	Grant-funded	Unit sale of product
Mode of accountability	Public	Private

determinant of the others. Although there is some tendency for the features in each of the two columns to occur together, this is not necessarily so, and in any case there is no obvious single line of causal determination between them. For this reason, all three dimensions will need to be treated as independent variables, and each as necessary to an adequate understanding of any particular bureaucratic organization.

Two further comments should be made about these differentiating principles. First, within each discipline there is a marked tendency to call the characteristics in the left-hand column bureaucratic and those in the right-hand one non-bureaucratic. According to the conceptual strategy adopted here, however, all organizations will be bureaucratic in so far as they conform to the general Weberian criteria of hierarchical rule-governed administration, etc.; and the differences will represent differences between bureaucratic types, rather than marking the boundary between the bureaucratic and the non-bureaucratic itself. Secondly, each pair does not necessarily represent a mutually exclusive alternative. We have already seen that there can be different degrees or combinations of mechanical and organic arrangements within the same organization. Similarly it is possible to find different methods of funding and modes of accountability also combined within one institution. But before we become submerged under an almost infinite complexity of bureaucratic types, it is important to stress that the task of theory is not so much to compile an exhaustive list of possibilities, as to identify the main determinants of organizational differentiation. Once equipped with these, the investigator should be able to understand the character and functioning of any particular bureaucratic organization, whatever its location on a spectrum of possibilities. To whom is it accountable and how? By what means is it financed? How is it structured in relation to its purpose and environment? These are the key questions to be asked, and none of them can be dismissed as irrelevant, or secondary.

The discussion of these key variables brings us directly to the question of administrative or organizational efficiency. As we have seen, the selection by each discipline of a particular variable is not accidental, but is related to its distinctive method of analysis, and conception of administrative efficiency. Organizational sociology is concerned with structure; efficiency is a question of how the organization is structured (how the division of labour is arranged, how precisely roles are defined, etc.), and the appropriateness of the structure to the organization's goals and environment. Political economy is concerned with finance, and takes its starting point from the pursuit of self-interest by individuals; efficiency is a question of so arranging the financial inducements and sanctions that the pursuit of individual self-interest serves to advance rather than hinder the goals of the organization. Public administration emphasizes an organization's culture and its mode of accountability; efficiency is a question of the appropriateness of its culture to the goals it pursues and to its particular method of accountability, and of the effectiveness with which individuals are socialized into acceptance of its normative order.

Do these different emphases offer mutually exclusive alternatives between which we must choose? Or can they be integrated into a more complete, and necessarily more complex, understanding? At first sight the approaches of political economy and public administration seem most obviously contradictory. After all, they are derived from the study of two contrasting institutions, market and state. Where the former is the arena for the pursuit of private advantage, from which the general interest results, if at all, only as unintended by-product, the latter concerns itself directly with the public welfare, and with the principles by which social life should be arranged and regulated. Assumptions about self-interest and normative order derive naturally from the study of each. Pressed to their logical conclusion, the two standpoints become contradictory, and deliver competing evaluations of public bureaucracy, critical and sympathetic respectively.

We have also seen, however, that neither perspective on its own can offer a coherent account even of its own subject. On the one hand, political economy requires reference to a normative order to make the concept of hierarchy intelligible; and the pursuit of self-interest within business firms is set within a framework of principles governing what is appropriate behaviour and remuneration for each position, and within an overall organizational ethos. On the other hand, norms of public service and administrative duty within a government bureaucracy are reinforced by gradations of status and privilege, and systematic procedures for individual reward and advancement. Furthermore, the effectiveness of both dimensions – normative order and the utilization of individual self-interest – cannot be divorced from a third: the way in which the division of labour within the institution is structured, and the scope it allows for individual initiative or discretion.

In conclusion, therefore, it should indeed be possible to advance beyond the differences of disciplinary perspective, as well as the differences between types of institution, to a more general theory of bureaucracy itself, combining three different dimensions of analysis: a structured division of labour, with a particular arrangement and definition of roles or offices; a normative order regulating the behaviour of its members, and internalized by them; a system of inducements and sanctions, directing the pursuit of individual self-interest. Just as no adequate account of bureaucracy, whether in general or particular, can be given without reference to all three dimensions, so the attainment of organizational efficiency or effectiveness will require attention to be given to them all, and to their interrelationship.

Bureaucracy and policy formation

So far this chapter has been concerned with administrative efficiency, and with models of bureaucracy which address the question of how far bureaucracies are efficient, or could be made more so. It should be evident from the discussion, however, that this question can only be answered by developing a systematic understanding of how bureaucracies actually function in practice; evaluation and explanation are interconnected, though the emphasis so far has been on the former. In the final section of the chapter I shall review some theories of bureaucracy with a more directly explanatory purpose, which can be derived from the models already considered. In order to focus the discussion, I shall concentrate on an issue that has concerned many writers on administration in the public sector: the influence of bureaucracy on the formation of policy. This is particularly an issue in the public sector, because of the complexity and publicly contested nature of its policy goals, though it has parallels in the private sector also.

One of the limitations to analyses of administrative efficiency is that they take the policies or goals of an organization as given, and concentrate on the question of how effectively they are carried out. But this is to treat administration as if it were simply a matter of implementing policies or goals already arrived at, and to overlook its contribution to their initial formulation. Although it is possible to draw a clear distinction between politicians and officials in terms of the method of their appointment and nature of their responsibility, the distinction does not so readily coincide with a line drawn between the formation and implementation of policy. Administrators, especially at their higher levels, typically act as advisors to politicians on policy. And since they usually have the advantage over a minister of greater experience and expertise in the policy area, at least collectively, their advice can be crucial in determining the content of that policy. After all, what *should* be done is dependent upon what *can*, and, if it can, upon what effects it will have, especially on other policies. Assessing such possibilities and consequences constitutes the distinctive expertise of officials, and is one of the sources of their influence. Apologists for bureaucracy see this influence as a matter of the rational assessment of the issues from case to case. Explanatory theories seek to show that it has a systematic tendency which derives from the character of bureaucracy itself.

These theories can for convenience be grouped according to the three models we have already considered, although they are not necessarily derived from them in a self-conscious manner. First, there are theories which explain policy in terms of bureaucratic interests, particularly its interests in secure employment, and in individual opportunities for increasing power, status or material reward. These hold that the systematic policy tendency of bureaucracy will be towards the protection and advancement of its own interests. The negative form of the theory holds that bureaucrats will oppose radical policies which threaten their own positions.

The most famous example of this argument was put forward by Robert Michels in his study of pre-First World War Social

Democracy in Europe, in which he attributed the deradicalization of the movement to the increase of bureaucratic posts as parties and unions extended their mass base, and to the fear of their incumbents that a revolutionary policy would jeopardize their livelihood. From this example Michels drew a general conclusion about the conservative bias of bureaucratic organization. However, even if he was correct in his analysis of European Social Democracy (see below, pp. 56–7) the wider conclusion does not follow, since it presupposes that radical policies will always threaten bureaucratic positions, and this is a matter that must surely depend upon the context. A public agency established for a limited purpose will be in danger of dissolution if it does not find new tasks to undertake, once its original purpose is completed; here bureaucratic interests will be on the side of innovation. And in government at large, where there is little threat of bureaucratic dissolution, whatever policies are adopted, it is difficult to explain any lack of radicalism in terms of bureaucratic interests alone. Indeed, the argument can go the other way. Since larger organizations produce higher pay and status for those at the top, senior bureaucrats have a vested interest in expansion, through either the extension of existing programmes, or the adoption of new ones. We have already met a version of this argument in the discussion of bureaucratic inefficiency, but it is important to distinguish between 'organizational slack' as a problem for the cost-effective execution of policy, and pressures for expansion which affect the nature of the policies themselves.

William Niskanen has argued over the course of a number of writings that the characteristic goal of bureaucrats is budget maximization, through the expansion of their department programmes. Like many political economists, however, he concludes that the resulting level of provision of public services will be 'too high' in comparison with some norm of market provision. This conclusion overlooks the fact that public provision is intended to meet a criterion of need as much as ability to pay, and that in any case state programmes have historically had to be supplemented by the market as a result of their inadequacy, rather than their surplus of provision over need. What is not in doubt is that electoral demand and bureaucratic interest combine to generate powerful pressures for the expansion of public services; but it is equally evident that such pressures are in turn constrained by the political limits on taxation and the administrative controls of a Treasury or Budget office.

The conjunction of a general bureaucratic disposition towards expansion, with the limitations imposed by finite resources, produces a different theory of bureaucratic interests which emphasizes the competition between different departments or agencies for their share of the budget. Such competition is not confined to the yearly bargaining round with the Treasury, but is felt across the whole range of policy. It is the nature of government policy that any proposal for change affects a number of departments or agencies simultaneously, and also differentially, in terms of its implications for the maintenance or expansion of their budgets. An extension of the road-building programme has consequences for bus and rail services; an expansion of nuclear power generation has implications for the coal industry, while a shift towards energy conservation affects both; changes in foreign policy or defence strategy have consequences for the relative importance of the different armed services, and so on. Any proposal to alter policy will find the bureaucratic interests of different departments or agencies engaged on different sides of the argument, and the outcome will depend on their respective weight, and on their ability to demonstrate that the policy which benefits their department is most in the public interest. This is the essence of what has come to be called the bureaucratic politics approach. It was originally developed in the foreign policy area, to counter the view that a nation's foreign policy could be explained according to the model of a single actor rationally calculating the most advantageous strategy, rather than as the outcome of contending interests within different bureaucratic agencies. The approach has subsequently been extended to other areas of policy.

Theories which explain political outcomes in terms of competition between contending interests need complementing two ways if they are to be at all plausible. One is through an examination of the structures which set the interests of different groups systematically in competition with one another, and determine their relative political weight. In the case of government bureaucracy, the way in which functions are divided between separate agencies or departments and between different tiers of government has significant consequences for the alignment of interests and the balance of political forces. Such an arrangement is in turn the accumulated product of a history of past policies, which become congealed in institutional form and develop a network of interests around them, both inside and outside the bureaucracy, which constrain present choices. It is this that makes incrementalism, the adding of the new to the old, the typical form of policy change. Existing structures also affect policy outcomes, not only through the alignment they give to competing interests in the influence of policy, but also through their consequences for its implementation. Policies which can only be implemented with great difficulty within existing structures, for example because they cut across the boundaries of established departments, have less chance of acceptance than those whose implementation is more straightforward. This explains the attraction for new governments of interdepartmental reorganization, especially where important new initiatives cut across existing boundaries.

Any explanation of policy in terms of competing bureaucratic interests, therefore, is incomplete without an examination of the structure within which they are located. But, secondly, it is also unintelligible without an understanding of the conventions which govern the expression of such interests, and which regulate the process of bureaucratic competition. As we have seen, bureaucracies possess well-developed cultures of their own, and the more so, the more self-enclosed their élite. These cultures embody elaborated codes governing the way administration is conducted, as well as larger assumptions about the world, which set their own limits to the range of policies considered possible or acceptable. Most state bureaucracies see themselves as guardians of a 'national interest' or 'interest of state' which transcends and outlasts the policies of particular governments. In the case of the British civil service, as is often pointed out, such conceptions are conditioned by an Oxbridge educated outlook of the gifted amateur or generalist, more attuned to the concerns of finance than of industry, and still attached to a great power role in an era of post-imperial decline. Such attitudes are not necessarily any more a conscious determinant of policy than are the administrative structures or limitations that render certain policy options unworkable; but they serve to define the parameters of what can be legitimately thought or seriously entertained.

If we add together these different theoretical explanations of what could be called bureaucratic policy – as the product of compromise between divergent bureaucratic interests, of the limitations imposed by administrative structures, of the tendencies of shared cultural assumptions – or, better, if we integrate them by showing how interests come to be aligned within a given administrative structure, and their expression defined by common cultures and beliefs: we then have a powerful argument that the content of policy, and not merely its execution, is systematically affected by the character of the administrative system. At its strongest, the argument holds that within bureaucracies, the relationship between means and ends becomes inverted; the nature of the administrative means determines the policy goal or end.

However, driving an argument to its logical conclusion does not necessarily ensure its validity. What this one ignores, manifestly, is the elected politician, with his or her own priorities. The idea that the minister has an essential role in policy-making cannot be so readily jettisoned, though the extent and effectiveness of that role will depend upon the individual, and upon the degree of his or her political support both inside and outside the government. Yet it is a mistake to see the typical relationship between politician and officials as one in which the former confronts the latter with policy ideas, which they then seek to divert or obstruct. If the explanations given above have any validity, it is much more a question of the politician providing an input of his or her own into the ongoing policy process, an input which can determine which of the competing internal factions prevail, or the precise balance of the compromise between them that is finally struck.

In any case, what the theories considered here show is that any analysis of bureaucracy as an instrument for the administration and implementation of policy has to be complemented by an analysis of its effects upon policy content. The discussion of the former necessarily has to make a sharp distinction between ends and means, between policy and its execution. Any evaluation of efficiency has to begin by taking ends as given. But this sharp distinction breaks down once the question of the formation of policy is placed upon the agenda. At this point the effect of the administrative system itself – its structure, interests and values – upon the content of policy, becomes significant. If we are to understand bureaucracy adequately, then it is in the complex interplay between its formative role in policy, and its translation of that policy into manageable directives at the front-line of the organization, that such an understanding is to be found.

Conclusion

I began the chapter with a number of sharply formulated distinctions. First was a distinction between the definitional, normative
and explanatory dimensions to a theory of bureaucracy. We have
seen that the sharpness of this distinction becomes blurred in
practice, not because the distinction itself is invalid, but because the
different dimensions are interrelated. Definitions of bureaucracy
tend to be governed by a particular conception of organizational
efficiency, and the latter in turn to be dependent upon a particular
mode of explaining how bureaucracies function. Second was a more
elaborated distinction between the models of bureaucracy developed within the disciplines of organizational sociology, political
economy and public administration respectively, and their very
different approaches to organizational analysis. These differences
of model-building in turn proved not to be absolute, or necessarily
antithetical, but complementary aspects to be integrated into a
more complete understanding of bureaucracy, and of the conditions
for organizational efficiency. Finally, the further distinction between ends and means, and the concept of administration as an
instrument for the execution of policy, which was necessary for any
discussion of bureaucratic efficiency, required revision in the light
of theories about the effects of the administrative system on the
content of policy itself.

At each point an initial distinction, necessary to the particular
stage of the argument, had to be transcended in order to reach a
fuller understanding of our subject, bureaucracy. But the reader
will not be surprised to learn that that understanding is not yet
complete, and not just for the trivial reason that we are still only in
Chapter 1. As the chapter has progressed, it should have become
evident that all the theories I have been discussing suffer from a
serious limitation. This is that they treat bureaucracy in isolation, as
a self-sufficient object of study, in abstraction from any social or
historical context, or any larger theory of society or history. This is
most obviously true of discussions of administrative efficiency,
which not surprisingly concentrate on the internal workings of
bureaucracy. But it is also true of the explanatory theories
considered, which, even where they are critical, see the influences
on policy as largely determined from within the administrative
system. They thus raise the question of bureaucratic power, and its

impact on policy, but are unable to identify the sources of that power within the wider society. In this emphasis they share some of the self-enclosed world of bureaucracy itself.

As I suggested in the Introduction, this self-enclosed quality is not accidental, in view of the origins and purpose of the disciplines under consideration. The academic subjects of organizational sociology, political economy and public administration have grown up in close relation to the practice of management, business and government respectively; they are concerned with the training of those who will occupy bureaucratic positions in these spheres; and their chief preoccupations, with how organizations function, and how they might be made more efficient, are those of administrators themselves, though they are mediated through the processes of academic enquiry, and in the terms of its discourse. Even political economy, which delivers a substantial critique of government bureaucracy, does so from the standpoint of business management. It is true that close proximity to the practice they study enables these disciplines to understand it from the inside – that is a source of insight as well as limitation – but we need to set bureaucracy in a larger context, and to see it from other, more critical, social perspectives. The next chapter will do this by considering the subject from the vantage point of a historical sociology. In the meantime, the conclusions of the present chapter must be regarded as provisional.

Note

1 M. Weber, *Economy and Society*, pp. 223, 973; *From Max Weber*, ed. H. Gerth and C.W. Mills, p. 214.

Theories of
Bureaucratic Power

Introduction

Towards the end of the previous chapter I argued that a major
limitation of a purely institutional approach to bureaucracy was its
inability to provide an adequate account of the nature and sources
of bureaucratic power. For such an account it is necessary to situate
bureaucracy within a larger social and historical context, and to
understand its function within the broadest social and political
processes, since it is from these that its power ultimately derives.
The present chapter will examine the theories of bureaucratic
power developed within two of the main schools of historical
sociology, the Weberian and Marxist respectively. The one,
Weberian, locates bureaucracy within a wider theory of authority
systems and their administration, and of the role and organization
of technical knowledge within industrial societies; it sees the power
of bureaucracy as deriving from the central place it occupies within
the historical process of modernization. The Marxist approach
locates bureaucracy within a wider theory of class domination and
class conflict, and sees its power as deriving from the function it
performs within a class society; it also situates it within a theory
of history which envisages the possibility of a future industrial
society without class divisions.

Both theories agree that the power of social groups and institutions
has to be understood in the light of the social function they perform
within an evolving historical process, but they disagree in their
respective accounts of this function and process. They also diverge in
terms of the standpoint from which they define bureaucratic power as

problematical. The Weberian standpoint is that of the liberal, non-bureaucratic élite, which sees its values threatened by the expansion of bureaucratic power: in particular, the values of individual freedom, and the scope for exceptional individuals to exercise a socially creative role in both economy and state. From this standpoint the solution to the problem of bureaucratic power lies in institutional arrangements which will ensure the control of bureaucracy *from above*, by non-bureaucratic élites. The Marxist standpoint is that of the potentially socialist working class, which is subordinate directly to bureaucratic control in economy and state. From this standpoint, any conflict between bureaucratic and non-bureaucratic élites is secondary, since both form part of one and the same system of class domination. And the solution to bureaucratic power can only come in the reconstitution of administrative structures in a post-class society, which ensures their subjection to democratic control *from below*.

The Weberian and Marxist theories of bureaucracy thus embody differences of social and political perspective, as well as differences of historical and sociological analysis. Each is related to a social position outside that of bureaucracy itself, and to corresponding political values that are critical of bureaucratic ideology and practice: in the one, those of a liberal élitism; in the other, those of a proletarian socialism. Their respective accounts of bureaucracy thus involve disputes not only about social structure and historical development, but between political values also, including contradictory assessments of capitalism and the possibility of socialism.

Weberian political sociology

Max Weber's model of bureaucracy has already been extensively treated in the previous chapter, and it may be asked why he is being considered further in the present one. The reason is that, however important his work has been to the sociology of organization, to confine a discussion of it to the terms of that discipline alone, and its preoccupation with bureaucratic functioning and organizational efficiency, is to narrow its focus unduly, and to remove it from the larger context of a theory of modern society and its development, to which it properly belongs. Within that larger context, Weber's concern was less with the question of organizational efficiency than with the expansion of bureaucratic power, and with the implications of that expansion for fundamental liberal values. From this standpoint he developed a theoretical analysis of bureaucracy that has been repeated and extended by many others through the course of the twentieth century. Weber left no organized school of followers behind him, but many sociologists have been influenced either directly or indirectly by his ideas. The concept 'Weberian' thus designates a recognizable theoretical tendency, reaching beyond the work of Weber himself.

The irreversible expansion of bureaucracy

That Weber should have given bureaucracy such a central place in his account of the development of modern society, or theory of modernization, is not accidental in view of the time and place in which his sociology was established. The first decade of the twentieth century saw the rapid cartelization and trustification of capitalist industry, and the growing employment of clerical, technical and managerial personnel within the individual enterprise. It also witnessed the expansion of the state into new areas of welfare provision and economic regulation, and the emergence of the mass political party. These developments, synonymous with the expansion of bureaucratic administration, had progressed furthest in Germany, which already possessed the most advanced type of bureaucracy in Europe, in the Prussian state. A distinctive conclusion of Weber's sociology was to define this process of bureaucratization, not as unique to Germany, or to its particular state form, but as a universal feature of modern society, and one which owed its development to the expanded administrative requirements, first of the modern state (the provision of a standing army, of a uniform system of law and taxation, etc.), and then of the capitalist enterprise. Because of its indispensability, bureaucratic administration was increasingly irreversible and escape-proof. It would be a sheer illusion, Weber wrote, 'to think for a moment that continuous administration can be carried out in any field except by means of officials working in offices . . . The choice is only between bureaucracy and dilettantism in the field of administration.'[1]

The development of bureaucratization was thus, in Weber's view, inseparably linked to the development of the territorial state and the capitalist economy, whose administrative needs could not be met by traditional means. Its development was also closely

linked to another typically modern process, that of democratization, in the sense of a levelling of traditional status differences, and
the opening of careers to talent. The degree of opening was of
course relative, since it required access to education to achieve the
certificates necessary for entry to a bureaucratic career. Yet the
pressures of democratization meant that administration could no
longer be preserved as the narrow privilege of traditional social
groups. And the development of a mass citizenship in turn
increased both the quantitative demands on the state administration, and the qualitative demand for uniformity of treatment,
which could only be met by a supra-local administrative system,
operating on the basis of impartiality between persons.

The idea of bureaucracy as the archetypically modern institution
was taken furthest in Weber's concept of rationalization, which
provided a kind of summation of the characteristics distinguishing
modern from traditional societies. When applied to bureaucracy,
the concept indicated far more than simply administrative efficiency, suggesting rather that its typical characteristics embodied
features that were integral to modern society itself. The derivation
of bureaucratic authority from precisely defined rules – governing
the criteria for appointment, the scope of authority and the conduct
of office – was the hallmark of modern authority as such, in contrast
to authority derived from tradition. The emphasis on specialist or
expert knowledge, as opposed to the all-round culture of the
educated gentleman, together with the rigorous calculation of the
most appropriate means to given ends, were underpinned by a
typically modern scientific culture or world view. And the idea of
work as duty, and the ethic of achievement, which sought to impose
a predictable order on the world, rather than merely adjust oneself
to it, derived from the Protestant ethic, which had deeply imprinted
itself upon the character of modern man. In these different respects,
bureaucracy could be seen as the most thoroughly rationalized
institution of the contemporary world.

As a system of administration, then, bureaucracy was in Weber's
view both an indispensable social formation and one which was
rooted in the most distinctive features of the modern world. At the
same time it constituted a formidable structure of power, and that
for the very reasons which made it such an effective system of
administration: its ability to coordinate action over a large area, its
continuity of operation, its monopoly of expertise and control of the

files, its internal social cohesion and morale. Its power confronted those both above and below it. To those above, to whom bureaucracy was formally subordinate, it posed the problem of how it could be effectively controlled by those who did not share its expertise. To those below, it constituted an immensely powerful structure of authority, which could readily control or outmanoeuvre them. The process of democratization, which had succeeded in levelling traditional distinctions of social rank, had created a more powerful authority system in their place. The only way for the subordinate to moderate its control was to create an organization of their own (interest group, trade union, political party), which would be subject to the same process of bureaucratization in its turn.

The inexorable expansion of bureaucracy, and hence of bureaucratic power, Weber saw as threatening to liberal values at a number of levels. Most directly, it constituted a threat to individual freedom. Weber recognized that the individualism characteristic of the classical period of liberal capitalism, which had rested upon individual self-financed activity, in business, politics or learning, was rapidly becoming a thing of the past, as the size of organizations took them beyond the reach of individual ownership. Indeed it was the very dynamic of individualism that had contributed to the expansion of capitalism, and hence in turn to bureaucratization; in this sense individualism had helped create the conditions for its own decline. Yet it was now a question of how it was possible to preserve any element of independent thought or action in the face of organizational structures, which constrained the individual by their discipline if a member, and through their wider social power if not. 'How is it at all possible', Weber wrote, 'in face of the overwhelming trend towards bureaucratization, to preserve any remnant of individual freedom of movement in any sense at all?'[2]

At a different level, bureaucratic power posed a challenge to the goal-determining function of those individuals who stood at the head of an organization. While Weber recognized an important role for officials in advising on policy, the distinction he drew between the choice of ends for an association, and the technical evaluation of means, was to him a fundamental one. The danger of bureaucratic power was not only that it would compromise the function of the organizational leader, particularly if the latter lacked relevant specialist knowledge, but that instrumental values would come to prevail in society at large, the logic of possible means over the assertion of ends. In particular, the values of order and security, nurtured in a bureaucratic environment, in which everything was precisely regulated, would come to prevail over the innovative, risk-taking approach of the industrial entrepreneur or political leader, schooled in the competitive and unpredictable environment of the economic or electoral market place. The world increasingly belonged to the 'men of order'. 'The central question', Weber wrote, 'is what we can oppose to this machinery, in order to keep a portion of humanity free from this pigeon-holing of the spirit, from this total domination of the bureaucratic ideal.'[3]

Such passages, in which Weber speaks of the 'iron cage' of a future bondage, seem deeply pessimistic. However, he saw the trend towards the total bureaucratization of life as a tendency only, not an inevitability. If bureaucratic administration was here to stay, the urgent question was what to *counterpose* to it – a formulation which Weber frequently repeated. One element in this idea of a 'contervailing power' was the characteristic liberal concern to limit power by creating a balance of social forces, in the tension or competition between which individual freedoms could be secured. In the contemporary world this suggested a pluralism of bureaucratic institutions, in different areas of social life with different social bases of support, such that there could be no monopoly or undue concentration of organizational capacity and specialist expertise in any one. A second element lay in securing the conditions for independent leadership, whether in the industrial or political sphere, which was capable of subjecting the power of officialdom to coherent direction and effective control. The following sections will examine the working out of these different aspects of the idea of countervailing power in two contexts: Weber's critique of socialism, and his theory of leadership democracy. Both will confirm the liberal standpoint from which his analysis of bureaucracy was developed. They will also show how that analysis in turn led to a reformulation of liberal theory in terms of a pluralist or competitive élitism, which has proved widely influential.

The socialist illusion

Weber's theory of bureaucracy provided the basis for a powerful critique of socialism. If the advance of bureaucratic administrative structures was irreversible, then socialist hopes of a future without

Herrschaft, without the domination of the majority by a minority, were illusory. The Marxist belief that the overthrow of capitalism would inaugurate the classless society was based upon the mistaken view that the private ownership of the means of production provided the sole basis for structures of minority rule. This was historically erroneous, and also overlooked the distinctively contemporary class-forming potential of technical knowledge and organizational power, necessary to a developed industrial society. The hierarchy to which the worker was subject at the workplace, Weber argued, was required by the organization of complex technical processes, and would therefore survive the abolition of private property. The expansion of administrative structures and personnel, which were growing faster than the proletariat, was a function of the increasing size and complexity of industrial enterprises, to which the issue of ownership was irrelevant. 'It is the dictatorship of the official', he concluded, 'not of the worker, that is, for the present at least, on the advance.'[4]

Indeed, the likelihood that socialism would produce a bureaucratic dictatorship was greatly increased by the demands that would be imposed upon a centralized administration. The creation of a planned system of production to meet social need, and the extension of equal citizenship from the formal rights of law and politics to the social and economic spheres, could only be met, Weber contended, by an enormous expansion of a central bureaucracy. At the same time the countervailing power structures that existed within capitalist society, in particular that of private capitalism itself, would be removed. Under private ownership the bureaucracies of government and industry could at least in principle counterbalance each other, and hold each other in check. Under socialism they would be forged together into a single all-embracing hierarchy, whose officials would become arbiters of the fortunes and welfare of all. Thus the unintended consequence of working class attempts to abolish the so-called 'anarchy of the market', and bring their social processes under conscious collective control, would be to put themselves under the sway of a more powerful, because more unified, hierarchy than before.

The idea that the institutions created by the working class to secure their emancipation would, through the process of bureaucratization, turn into agencies to perpetuate their own subordination, was also the theme of Robert Michels' work on political parties. On the basis of his analysis of West European Social Democracy, Michels concluded that the bureaucratic positions within party and trade union had become a principal avenue for the social advancement of energetic and talented members of the working class, who abandoned any revolutionary aims for their class once their own social revolution was accomplished. According to his analysis, prospective revolutionaries confronted an insoluble dilemma: either to create an organization, and see their goals subverted from within, or abandon permanent organization like the anarchists, and remain ineffectual. However, Michels' insistence upon the universally conservative character of organization led him to overlook the possibility that in a revolutionary movement or party which was not fully bureaucratized, such as the Bolshevik party, the revolutionary commitment of its leadership might be sustained to the point of a violent overthrow of the old regime. It was this eventuality that Weber himself addressed with his contention that all revolutions in modern times, even those most anti-bureaucratic in inspiration, could only succeed in confirming and extending the existing bureaucracy, because of its indispensability for consolidating their hold on power. This political necessity, combined with the centralizing thrust of its socialist purpose, could only ensure the rise of a new dictatorship from revolutionary socialism.

If one strand to Weber's critique of socialism concerned the consequences for individual freedom which he believed would follow from the abolition of independent power centres capable of checking a centralized bureaucracy, a second concerned the implications for the economy of replacing the capitalist entrepreneur, working within a competitive market, by an industrial manager subject to the requirements of a central plan. Following debates about the experience of centralized planning in the wartime German economy, Weber argued that the abandonment of the market would leave economic planners without the information necessary for the calculation of prices, and hence for the efficient allocation of the factors of production. In the sense of ensuring the maximum calculability of economic operations, the market was more rational than a system of central planning. Moreover, the demise of entrepreneur, whose innovative role was supported by the competitive pressures of the market, would remove the major source of dynamism within the economy, in exchange for the bureaucratic priorities of order and security. At a certain stage of

economic development, he argued, the state bureaucracy had been
a force for economic expansion, through facilitating the extension
of the market, and the assault on traditional social privileges. But
the more it came to encroach upon the market, the more it turned
into a force for economic stagnation.

Weber's prognostications for a socialist society, in short, were
gloomy. The combination of bureaucratic power and bureaucratic
order threatened to create a society as subservient as that of ancient
Egypt and as stagnant as the late Roman Empire, albeit on a
technically much more advanced basis. Although Weber died in
1920, before the full consequences of the Bolshevik revolution had
become clear, later Weberians have contended that the subsequent
history of the Soviet Union fully vindicated his analysis. In particular, the idea that the revolution had thrown up a new bureaucratic
ruling class, coordinated and disciplined by the institution of the
Communist Party, soon became a commonplace. The works of
writers such as Bruno Rizzi (*The Bureaucratization of the World*) or
James Burnham (*The Managerial Revolution*), at the end of the
1930s, were distinctly Weberian in their analysis of the power basis
of this new class in the controlling position which its administrative
and managerial skills gave it within both industry and government.
Weberian too was their scepticism about the possibility of the
working class ever achieving through its political struggle what no
other subordinate class had achieved throughout history: the abolition of class rule, rather than victory for a new ruling class.

However, there is an important difference to be drawn between
disillusioned Marxist revolutionaries such as Burnham and Rizzi,
and Weber, in that the latter never shared the condemnation of
capitalist society which made the Soviet Union appear simply as a
parallel system of exploitation to capitalism. Burnham and Rizzi
both defined the USSR as just a more developed example of the
replacement of a capitalist class by a managerial or bureaucratic one
– more developed, because the process had happened there through
revolutionary overthrow, rather than via the gradual replacement
of ownership by control that was taking place in the West. Weber's
theory, in contrast, for all its admission that bureaucratization was a
universal feature of modern societies, set clear limits to any conver-
gence thesis by its insistence that capitalist societies were distinguished by a pluralism of competing bureaucratic organizations,
and by the subordination of its bureaucracies to non-bureaucratic

élites. It was precisely this insistence upon the élite pluralism of capitalist societies that distinguished élite theorists of liberal provenance (Weber, Mosca and Pareto) from those originating as disillusioned revolutionaries, who were brought up to view such pluralism as more apparent than real, and for whom therefore any distinction between the Soviet Union and the West was to prove insubstantial.

The difference between Weber's theory of bureaucratic rule and the later one of Rizzi and Burnham was most marked at the point where the latter argued that the rise of bureaucracy to supremacy resulted from the superiority of planning over the market, whether in the form of Fascist corporatism, the Soviet five-year plans, or the New Deal in the USA. Here Weber's position was much closer to that of von Mises or von Hayek, who used evidence from the USSR to support their general theoretical arguments against economic planning at the level of a whole economy. Von Mises' early article on the impossibility of rational calculation in a planned economy had in fact been published by Weber shortly before his death. But it is reasonable to suppose that Weber would also have agreed with von Hayek's more philosophical argument about the inherent unpredictability of economic life, to which the decentralized entrepreneur was much better able to adjust than a centralized planner, since this argument accorded with a basic assumption of Weber's own sociology. This was the so-called 'paradox of consequences': the idea that the consequences of social action often diverge from, or even contradict, its intention, because of the responses it induces in other social agents who are affected by it.

According to this principle, the idea of rationally planning a whole economy or society is essentially contradictory, because the planners can never sufficiently predict or control the responses of those whose cooperation is necessary to make their plans effective. If such a conclusion undermines the optimistic hope of bringing all social processes under conscious human control (the 'end of pre-history', as Marx called it), it also precludes the most pessimistic scenarios of totalitarian theory, which envisage the whole of a society as automata operating at the behest of a centralized bureaucracy. Bureaucratic control is certainly possible in the sense of stifling individual freedom; it is much less so in the sense of achieving the economic or social outcomes that bureaucrats intend. This is one of those 'irrationalities' of the rationalization process that Weber himself was so quick to point out.

In conclusion, the analysis of the former Soviet Union that derives from Weber's work avoids the crude liberal simplification which sees the bureaucratic dictatorship as simply the product of a personal power striving on the part of individuals. According to the Weberian view, the dominance of the bureaucratic structure derived from the indispensability of its social function in a planned economy, and from the powers and privileges that accrued to this function, in the absence of any countervailing power. It was the outcome of a principled, though misguided, socialist purpose, and could not be attributed simply to the unfavourable circumstances in which the socialist project was first attempted. Only in a capitalist system, in the Weberian view, can bureaucratic domination be avoided, though even here the bureaucratic state poses a threat to individualism, as the final section will show.

The theory of leadership democracy

Weber's political theory was developed in the context of the Wilhelmine state system, in which government ministers were usually appointed from the ranks of the civil service, and were responsible to the Kaiser rather than to parliament. As a result of the personal limitations of the Kaiser on the one side, and the lack of effective parliamentary accountability on the other, the civil service had come to occupy the dominant position within the state. It was a system, not merely of bureaucratic administration, but of bureaucratic *rule*. As such, Weber believed, it severely exposed the limitations of officials, once they exchanged an administrative function for a political role to which they were not suited. For all the superiority of bureaucracy as a means of administration, the orderly, rule-governed activity of the official provided no schooling in the qualities required of a politician: the readiness to assume personal responsibility for policy; to mobilize public support for it, and defend it against opposition; to risk losing office in the event of serious failure or loss of support. The erratic course of German policy in the pre-war and wartime periods, Weber believed, resulted from the lack of a publicly accountable leadership, and demonstrated what the most perfect bureaucracy could *not* achieve.

In Weber's view, the tendency of bureaucracy to exceed its

administrative function and assume a political role was an inherent danger, stemming from its control over official knowledge and an ideology which promoted the values of administration over politics. Professional administrators typically compared the amateurism of the politician unfavourably with their own specialist expertise; the talking shop of parliament unfavourably with the achievements of administrative action; the conflicts of party and sectional interests unfavourably with their own representation of the general interest in society and state. Such contrasts were reinforced by a token parliamentary system, whose members were denied responsibility for policy, and reduced to ineffectual gesture politics. For this reason Weber was at the forefront of demands for the democratization of the German constitution.

But how exactly would democratization provide an antidote to bureaucratic power? At this point Weber's study of contemporary developments in electoral and party politics, in Britain and elsewhere, proved significant. He noted how the extension of the suffrage was transferring power from local notables to the party machines, which were capable of organizing electoral campaigns on a national basis. At the same time the individual parliamentary representative was declining in importance, in favour of the party leader, whose personality was becoming increasingly decisive even for the election of other party members. Elections were turning into a vote of confidence in the capacity of individual leaders, i.e. a form of plebiscite which gave them considerable control over their party and wide scope for the individual determination of policy. Such leaders, Weber argued, hardened on the battlefield of electoral politics and sustained by a popular legitimacy, could provide a decisive counterweight to the state bureaucracy, through their ability to subject it to political direction and control.

This theory of leadership democracy acknowledged a decline in the importance of parliament, even within parliamentary systems, as a result of the process of bureaucratization in party and state. Not only was the individual parliamentarian becoming less important in comparison with the party and its leader; some of the representative function of parliament was also being surrendered, as organized interests lobbied the executive directly through their contacts in the relevant ministries. At the same time, however, Weber stressed the significance of those parliamentary functions that remained: the public review of the executive, particularly through the work of specialist committees; the selection and training of future political leaders; the provision of a mechanism for their removal if they lost public confidence. If the process of bureaucratization in party and state came to limit the role of parliament, and necessitate a revision of classical parliamentary theory, it also increased the importance of those functions that remained.

Democratization, then, according to Weber, signified no great dispersal of power to the masses, nor any substantial control over policy by the people. Such ideas were illusory in the bureaucratic age. What it signified was, first, the selection of leaders by electoral competition, which gave them the legitimacy to impose their own direction on the bureaucracy; and, secondly, the provision through parliament of a forum for public debate and review of policy, and a mechanism for removing leaders in the event of a serious loss of confidence. This theory is very similar to that later popularized by Joseph Schumpeter in his work *Capitalism, Socialism and Democracy*, whose definition of democracy as a mechanism for the selection and legitimation of leaders has been often quoted. There is little doubt that Schumpeter had been influenced by Weber in the development of his theory. The criticism often made of both, that their conception of leadership democracy shows no evidence of any commitment to the democratic values of political equality or popular participation, though correct, is beside the point, since neither claimed to espouse such values in the first place. Their theory was entirely liberal in its inspiration.

Central to this liberal perspective, for Weber at least, was the belief in the creative historical and social force of the individual, and the view that collectivities formed at most a means for effecting (and also frustrating) the visionary purpose of individuals. They could play no initiating role on their own. If the growth of bureaucratization had brought to an end the classic era of individualism, through destroying the independence of self-financed activity, at the same time it created the possibility for exceptional individuals to give effect to their personal inspiration at the head of organizations – a kind of individualism writ large – provided that the processes of social selection encouraged them to reach that far. The significance of the theory of leadership democracy was that it revealed the mechanism for the emergence of such individuals in the competition and legitimation of the electoral process. It also confirmed the role of the mass as that of a following, who should be discouraged from encroaching upon the independence of their leaders. Such was in effect the essence of Weber's much disputed concept of charismatic authority, and of the sharp antithesis he drew between the routines of bureaucracy and the innovative force of charisma.

The importance of Weber to any discussion of bureaucracy, in conclusion, lies in the fact that he grasped sooner than anyone the implications of the expansion of bureaucratic administration, which, though only emerging in his time, have taken the remainder of the century to work themselves out, in the history of the former USSR and the western democracies alike. Secondly was the liberal standpoint from which he charted the growth of bureaucratic power, and defined it as threatening to both individual freedom and the independence of non-bureaucratic élites. Finally, in his critique of socialism and conception of leadership democracy, he showed how the solution to the problem lay in a substantial revision of the classical liberal conception of limited or countervailing power, whether in the competition between different bureaucratic organizations, or in the separate power base of the political leader in the popular legitimacy of the electoral process.

There is a significant congruence to be observed here between Weber's social standpoint, his political values and his mode of sociological analysis. The non-bureaucratic élites whose position he saw as threatened or circumscribed by bureaucratic advance have been the main bearers of liberal values in modern society. And liberalism's traditional concern with the power of formal organizational and political hierarchies was reflected in a Weberian political sociology which gave central place to the analysis of such hierarchies, and defined bureaucracy as the key institution of the modernization process. Marxist theory reveals a similar congruence between agency, values and mode of analysis, but in a different direction, as an examination of its theory of bureaucratic power will make clear.

Marxist political economy

With the collapse of Communism in 1989, and of most of the regimes inspired by the Soviet system, Marxism as a social theory has entered a phase of crisis. This is true even of those forms of Marxism, examined here, which were critical of the Soviet Union as a distortion of socialism, or as a new form of class oppression. This is

because since 1989 any viable, let alone desirable, alternative to
capitalism, such as Marxism espouses, has seemed merely Utopian.
At most, it would seem, socialism can only be realized within
capitalism, as social democracy, rather than as an outright alternative to it.

Why then should we continue to study Marxism? The reason is
the same as that when it was first developed: it offers a particularly
forceful analysis and critique of capitalism as an economic system.
Such an analysis is no less relevant now that capitalism appears
triumphant, trade unions are subdued, and all alternatives are off
the political agenda. Indeed, the current phase of capitalism under
its neo-liberal political managers bears many of the hallmarks which
Marx first identified as distinctive of the capitalism of his time: the
constant revolutionizing of the means of production; the pen-
etration of market competition into all corners of the globe and all
spheres of social life; the coexistence of widespread unemployment
and insecurity with unmet social needs; the intensification of
economic inequalities, both within countries and between them;
and so on. As long as capitalism continues, and provokes collective
struggles to contain or reverse its most damaging consequences,
Marxist analyses will continue to offer an important alternative,
both to Weberian sociology and to the orthodox political economy
considered in the previous chapter, including their analyses of
bureaucracy.

The standpoint from which Marxists approach the analysis of
bureaucracy is that of the working class and its subordination within
a capitalist system of production. This subordination is primarily to
capital itself, and only secondarily to a particular administrative
structure, whether in industry or state. Understanding this subordination, and the possibility for modifying or overcoming it, is
consequently the task of a critical political economy rather than a
political sociology; and bureaucracy takes second place as an object
of study to the analysis of class relations. Moreover, since any
improvement in the position of the working class, let alone an end to
its subordination, can only come through collective action, rather
than individual endeavour, this is a standpoint which embraces
collective or socialist values rather than individualist ones. From
such a standpoint, the problem of power structures is how to subject
them to democratic control, rather than how to preserve room for
individual freedom or the creativity of exceptional talents.

There is no systematic treatment of bureaucracy in the Marxist tradition in the way that there is in the Weberian. This is partly for the reason already mentioned, that Marxism sees administrative structures as secondary to class relations. But it is also that Marxist theory originated in the mid-nineteenth century, before the dramatic expansion of bureaucracy, and that its treatment of the subject, and indeed its concept of bureaucracy itself, has developed piecemeal. Marx used the term bureaucracy in the typical nineteenth-century sense which associated it with a particular type of state, in contrast to parliamentary systems. In the first decades of the twentieth century, Marxists came to regard bureaucracy as the general form of state administration in capitalist society, whatever the political system, and linked it to the growth of imperialism and monopoly capital. A later generation of Marxists in the 1930s was confronted with the problem of explaining the rise of the bureaucratic state in the post-revolutionary, non-capitalist society of the USSR. And it is only comparatively recently that Marxists have dealt with bureaucracy as a phenomenon outside the state, whether in industry or society more generally, along the lines of the Weberian conception. These different episodes, or dimensions of the subject, have never been properly synthesized, either in a general theory of state bureaucracy in capitalist and non-capitalist societies, or in a theory that links bureaucratic administration in both economy and state. Yet the potential for such a synthesis is present within Marxist theory, which, like orthodox political economy, provides a simple yet powerful explanatory model, capable of linking together the most wide ranging social and political phenomena, though of course it does not accept the orthodox starting point in an unchanging conception of human nature. In what follows I shall attempt to draw some of these elements together in a systematic, rather than historical, account of the Marxist theory of bureaucracy.

Capitalism and bureaucracy

As with the discussion of orthodox political economy in the previous chapter, any treatment of Marxism must begin at the beginning, only moving on to bureaucracy at the appropriate stage of the argument. The starting point of Marxist analysis is the proposition that production to satisfy material needs is the most basic activity of any society, and that understanding the way production is organized, and the social relations within which it is carried on, provides the key to understanding society as a whole. All historical societies since the earliest communal ones have featured a dominant class which, through the ownership and control of some necessary means of production, has been able to extract and appropriate from a class of direct producers a surplus product beyond what is necessary for the latter's own subsistence and reproduction. On the basis of this surplus, the dominant class has been able to sustain activities, a lifestyle and a culture, that are radically different from those of the direct producers. This process of extracting and appropriating a surplus is called exploitation. Just as the activities of production are the most basic, so the relation between dominant and subordinate class constitutes the most fundamental power relation of a society, which other social institutions serve to sustain. However – and this constitutes the limit to any historical generalization in Marxism – different historical systems or modes of production differ radically from one another in the way in which the surplus product is extracted and appropriated from the direct producers, and in the precise relationship that results between the system of production and other social institutions.

The distinctive feature of the capitalist system of production is that the relationship between the dominant and subordinate classes is established through a market exchange, and on the basis of a formal legal equality, rather than through a legally defined and enforced inferiority, as in a slave or serf society. The subordination of labour to capital is determined by the historical fact that the working class has no means of subsistence of its own, and is driven by economic necessity to sell its labour power to capital for a wage. This exchange, equal in appearance only, gives the capitalist the right to control the worker, and to extract and appropriate surplus labour beyond that necessary to produce the value of the worker's wages. This surplus labour is the source of capitalist profit. Because capitalists are also in competition with each other, they are under continual pressure to minimize the cost of labour, and extract the maximum output from it. Workers for their part will resist this pressure, since it operates to their disadvantage and to the benefit of capital. Capitalist production is thus characterized by endemic conflict between the two classes over the conditions and pace of work, the length of the working day, the relative distribution of the product, etc. The system of private property makes decisions about all these issues into a struggle between classes.

To recognize the capitalist system of production as a system of class exploitation and class conflict is, for the Marxist, the starting point for any adequate understanding of the institutions of capitalist society. For example, as Marx himself insisted, the management structure in the capitalist enterprise serves not only to coordinate the different elements of the production process, but also as a means of class discipline and control; it is needed to secure the extraction of surplus labour on behalf of capital, and to regulate the resulting class conflict. It performs a class-regulating function as well as a purely technical or administrative one. Those who fail to understand the class nature of capitalism see only the latter function, and conclude that the expansive hierarchical apparatus of management is required by the sheer complexity of organizing industrial production under whatever system of ownership. What this overlooks is the capitalist pressure to extract the maximum labour from its workforce, and the collective resistance this pressure provokes, which together necessitate an apparatus of supervision and control, not merely one of coordination; and the greater the resistance, the more powerful the apparatus has to be.

This simple observation of Marx holds the key to the developed Marxist theory of bureaucracy, whether in economy or state. For the Marxist, bureaucracy comprises a system of administration, or rather those elements in a system of administration, which serve the function of class control and the containment of class conflict. If we stay with the management of the capitalist enterprise for the moment, we can see at once where such a theory contradicts others we have already looked at. It challenges the Weberian thesis that bureaucratic administration is required simply by the technical complexity of modern production, since this ignores its central class function. Distinctive elements of bureaucracy, which make it into a formidable and self-enclosed structure of power, such as its secrecy, its monopoly of knowledge and organizational initiative, its social cohesion and superiority, not to mention its sheer extent, derive from this function, rather than its purely coordinating one. The Marxist account challenges, secondly, theories of the 'managerial revolution', whether in the critical version that the managerial class exploits labour in its own right, or the apologetic version which

presents the managerial corporation as serving the public interest
rather than the maximization of profit. To the Marxist, the structure
and activities of management are subordinate to the logic of
capitalist profit, and cannot be analysed independently of the
capital-labour relationship from which they derive. Going further,
the Marxist theory also challenges the view within orthodox
political economy that the hierarchy of supervision and control is
the consequence of an innate propensity in human nature to
shirking, and that the origin of entrepreneurial profits lies in the
rewards that accrue to successful supervision. Such a view puts the
cart before the horse, by making ownership the consequence,
rather than the cause, of the need to control a recalcitrant
workforce. Finally, Marxism questions the preoccupation of organizational sociology with efficiency, as if this were a neutral concept
presupposing community of interest within an organization, when
the question must be: efficiency for whom, and at whose expense?

It is useful to begin a discussion of the Marxist theory of
bureaucracy with industrial management, since this is the point
where its class function is most directly evident. The state bureaucracy requires a more complex analysis, though this is the site of
Marx's own earliest discussions of administration. From the outset
Marx challenged the Hegelian idea that the state bureaucracy
represented the universal interests of society, above the particularism of class interests. He argued instead that the state institutions
served the interests of the class which was dominant in society, or a
combination of such classes where the society was in a process of
transition from one system of production to another. In a predomi-
nantly capitalist society, this did not necessarily mean that the
bureaucracy was under the direct control of the capitalist class,
either formally through their representatives in government, or
informally through their use of financial power to manipulate the
government from behind the scenes, though both these were indeed
possible. The example of the Bonapartist state of Napoleon the
Third, with its massive bureaucracy rising high above society,
capital included, convinced Marx that a regime could serve the
interests of capital by guaranteeing the general conditions of order
and property necessary to its continued activity and expansion. A
distinctive feature of capitalist production was that the extraction of
surplus labour and the expansion of capital were achieved by a
purely economic, not a political, process, and within the sphere of

civil society, not the state. Capitalists did not therefore require their own control of the state, since guaranteeing order and the rights of property constituted the basic rationale of the state apparatus itself. In securing these rights for all, the bureaucracy was in fact serving the interests of capital, and underwriting its dominance within civil society. And when the working class organized to resist its own exploitation, it could only appear as mounting a sectional challenge to the general rights of property and posing a threat to order, which the state apparatus was bound to resist. In doing so the bureaucracy could readily believe it was representing the universal interest.

Marx's analysis of Bonapartism supports that tendency in Marxist theorizing which holds that it is more important to investigate what the state institutions actually do, why they do it and with what consequences, rather than to ask who occupies the bureaucratic posts, and what their social background happens to be. The latter may indicate how meritocratic recruitment is, but provides an inadequate explanation for bureaucratic performance. Since Marx's time, state bureaucracies in the West have undergone a massive expansion, under the pressure of two divergent forces. The first derives from the needs of capitalist production itself, and the increasingly substantial tasks it requires the state to undertake at society's expense to ensure its profitability: the provision of a material infrastructure, training a skilled workforce, financing scientific research, regulating the economy, and so on. The second derives from the process of democratization, and the demands it imposes upon social order. In Marx's time, before the expansion of the suffrage, the working class was subordinated by a combination of coercive and ideological control. Once democratic institutions were conceded under working class pressure, coercion had to give way to the mobilization of consent, and the state was forced to concede demands for social legislation in the fields of health, housing, welfare, trade union rights, etc., which went well beyond the requirements of capitalist reproduction. These divergent pressures currently involve the state in conflicting tasks: on the one hand it must maintain the conditions for capitalist profitability, on which the economy and its own finances depend; on the other it must maintain the support of the working class for the social order, which requires levels of state spending and redistributive policies that repeatedly threaten capitalist profitability itself. These conflicting tasks generate contradictory pressures within the state administration, which are experienced both within and between the different bureaucratic agencies.

Parts of the above account may seem distinctly Weberian. After all, Weber's explanation for the growth of state bureaucracies lay in the quantitative expansion and qualitative complexity of administrative tasks required by the technical advance of industry and the process of democratization respectively. Obviously there is some measure of agreement over this. From the Marxist standpoint, however, Weber takes no account of the class dimension to these tasks: of the way in which securing the conditions for capitalist profitability introduces elements of social control into the heart of the welfare state. This is most evident in those agencies responsible for administering social security. Unemployment, in the Marxist view, is itself in part the product of capitalist labour-shedding in the search for increased profitability, and also a means to put pressure upon those in employment to accept revision of working practices, intensified work rates, etc. It is a prime means for the social control of labour. But it can only be so if social security levels are set at a point which do not threaten work discipline, and if entitlements are rigorously policed. Provision of individual needs takes second place to the enforcement of labour discipline. In view of this function, it is hardly surprising that social security administration should be among the most bureaucratic of all welfare agencies, as those subject to it are only too well aware.

The degree to which the welfare state's overall provision for individual needs is incompatible with its controlling and servicing function for capital is partly determined by the general state of the economy. In a period of recession, when profits are squeezed, the social legislation achieved in more expansive times becomes a luxury that can no longer be afforded. Particularly vulnerable are the collective rights of trades unions, and those aspects of the welfare state which do not contribute directly to the needs of capitalist production. This is the meaning of demands for efficiency and cutting out waste. At the same time there are moves to contract out state services to private enterprise, and introduce business management practices into those that remain, to ensure the more intensive exploitation of the workforce. From above, this is termed reducing bureaucracy. To those below, however, it means increasing it, since the administration becomes more hierarchical, the discipline more intense, and the control over work practices more detailed. In these different ways, the class-policing element in welfare administration becomes more marked.

Such changes do not take place without corresponding shifts in the state itself at the highest level, depending upon the degree of working class resistance they provoke. Typically this involves a shift of emphasis from social welfare to the directly coercive institutions of the state, and a strengthening of the executive arm at the expense of the representative one. How far such a process goes depends upon political as well as economic factors, such as the capacity of established political parties to maintain their social following in the face of welfare cuts, and the degree of legitimacy of the parliamentary order itself. In countries where the recession bites particularly deep, where the class struggle is especially intense, and where democratic institutions enjoy only a limited or conditional legitimacy, social order can only be guaranteed by the executive making itself supreme above parliament, in some form of dictatorship. If in normal circumstances the bureaucracy has to limit democratic control to carry out its class regulative function, in exceptional circumstances of acute class struggle it may have to raise itself above democratic institutions altogether. At such moments, as Marx argued in his analysis of Bonapartism, even capital has to abandon its political representation in favour of a strong figure who will guarantee order and property. The fact that, under a dictatorship of this sort, the bureaucracy itself may be subject to the direction of a powerful leader enjoying popular legitimacy, reveals the limitation of the Weberian perspective, which considers only the relations between the bureaucracy and the political leader, and not the possible subordination of society at large to both.

According to Marxist theory, in conclusion, the development of bureaucracy as a formidable structure of power, which to Weberians is inseparable from the administrative requirements of a complex industrial society, is rather the product of its class regulative function under capitalism, which reaches its apogee in the bureaucratic or Bonapartist state. Bureaucracy combines both coordinating and class functions; it is the latter that is responsible for its most distinctively bureaucratic features. It follows that administration in a post-class society will lose its bureaucratic character. What precisely does this mean? Not the idea of Saint-Simon, that the government of men will be replaced by the administration of things, which was always an oversimplification. As Engels argued, coordination requires both authority and clearly defined rules; trains have to run according to a fixed timetable, and the passengers have to obey the railway staff. However, it would be a form of authority which was readily subject to popular control and accountability. The difference would be that between policemen regulating traffic, and forcibly dispersing a workers' picket. The former exercise authority by agreement; the latter requires a concentration of power and a degree of secrecy that will elude popular control.

If such is to be the character of administration in a post-capitalist society, an obvious question presents itself. Why was it that, in the first attempted post-capitalist society, the USSR, the bureaucratic state raised itself beyond popular control to a degree rarely attained before?

Bureaucratic degeneration of the proletarian revolution

Few revolutionary Marxists anticipated that a bureaucratic administration would survive into the post-revolutionary society, let alone become the dominant force within party and state. Explanations for this development became a matter of necessity, as well as providing a touchstone for different political positions and attitudes towards the Soviet Union. One of the most influential analyses remains that of Trotsky, whose writings of the late 1920s and 1930s (especially *The Revolution Betrayed*) charted the way the bureaucracy had come to replace the proletariat as the leading force, first within the party, and then over society at large. This process had a dual aspect: the rise of bureaucratic power on one side, and the decline of a proletarian democracy capable of checking it, on the other. According to Trotsky, both aspects had their roots in a single cause: the backwardness and underdevelopment of Russian society.

It should be said that the backwardness of Russian society had always been used by Marxists of a reformist tendency as an argument against the Bolshevik revolution having been attempted at all. Writers such as Kautsky argued from the first that the attempt to create socialism in a society lacking the material and cultural preconditions for it could only result in an overweening state having to force a historically premature project upon a reluctant population. From this perspective the bureaucratization of the revolution came as no surprise. To Trotsky and other Bolsheviks, however, the degeneration of the revolution was not inscribed in the Bolshevik project at the outset, but resulted from the isolation of the Soviet Union through the failure of the Social Democratic parties of Western Europe, in particular Germany, to take advantage of the revolutionary moment at the end of the war, a failure to which Kautsky's reformism itself notably contributed. Once isolated from any international revolution, and cast in upon its own pitiful resources, the Soviet Union could only develop in a bureaucratic direction.

What precisely was the connection between bureaucratism and underdevelopment, according to Trotsky? The key to it lay in a statement of the young Marx: 'A development of the productive forces is the absolutely necessary practical premise [of Communism], because without it want is generalized, and with want the struggle for necessities begins again, and that means that all the old crap must revive.'[5] The more impoverished the society, the more intense would be the struggle for existence, and the more urgent the need of a 'policeman' to keep order. Such was the condition of the Soviet Union in the aftermath of the civil war, and this was the key to the power of the bureaucracy as the chief instrument of social control. In fulfilling this function, the bureaucracy had to raise itself above the masses in order to exert control over them; in so doing it became 'the chief planter and protector of inequality'[6] through its own privileges, whose defence became a source of further alienation from the masses, and a further reason for having to reinforce its control.

If one aspect of the dual process of bureaucratization lay in the degree of material scarcity, and the bitterness of individual and social struggle it engendered, the other aspect was provided by the cultural impoverishment of the Russian people, which made it difficult to sustain a vigorous proletarian democracy as a check on bureaucratic growth. 'Formed in the barbarous circumstances of Tsarism,' Trotsky observed, 'the Russian people were anything but made to order for the demands of a socialist revolution.'[7] Marx's theory that the revolutionary process would itself be the chief educator of the proletarian masses had been borne out by the vigorous intra-party democracy of the revolutionary period. But with the destruction of the most energetic elements of the proletariat in the civil war, and the exhaustion of those who remained, the limitations of the human material available to continue the revolutionary process were exposed. As the bureaucracy expanded, attracting to itself the most able cadres, the masses were pushed away from active participation in the party and its leading role in society. And as democracy withered, so the creative impetus of open debate and the free flow of ideas gave way to bureaucratic conservatism, checking the process of socialist advance.

Trotsky's contention that bureaucracy and social harmony are inversely proportionate was entirely consistent with the Marxist theory of bureaucracy developed from the analysis of its role within capitalist society, as an instrument of social control. Yet it performed this function there, not independently in its own right, but in the interests of the dominant social class of capital. On whose behalf, then, did the Soviet bureaucracy exercise its controlling function?

Trotsky's answer to this question was a complex one. Insofar as the bureaucracy maintained intact the major achievement of the revolution – the public ownership of the means of production – which formed the economic basis for the advance towards socialism, it acted as a substitute for the proletariat, in much the same way as Bonapartism had defended the social and economic interests of capital, while dominating it politically, and feeding off it in parasitic fashion. The bureaucratic state constituted a transitional political form between capitalism and socialism, when the capitalist class had been defeated, but the proletariat was too weak to act on its own behalf. On the other hand, in so far as the bureaucracy had re-established bourgeois norms of distribution and inequality, it contained the possibility of a reversion to capitalism, through the consolidation of its privileges into a system of private ownership. Which of these two possibilities was realized depended, in Trotsky's view, upon the prospects for a second, political revolution by the proletariat to displace the bureaucracy from its dominant position – a possibility which depended in turn upon the prospects for proletarian revolution in the West.

To some of Trotsky's followers and many of his critics, this analysis of the social basis of bureaucracy looked less like a theoretical complexity than a contradiction. As time passed, the idea of the Soviet regime as an unstable and transitory one seemed less and less plausible. And the view that it still constituted a workers' state, albeit a degenerated one, seemed meaningless when the working class was effectively denied any political rights in its own state. It was much simpler to conclude that the domination of the bureaucracy comprised, not a transition point between capitalism and socialism, but a new form of class society in which the bureaucracy had established itself on the backs of the proletariat as a new ruling class. Yet this conclusion in turn had serious implications not only for the Marxist theory of class, but also for the political attitude to be taken towards the USSR and other Communist countries. Whether the Soviet bureaucracy was defined as a ruling class or merely a new political stratum thus became a matter of considerable controversy among Marxist writers.

Those who argued that the bureaucracy constituted a political stratum rather than a class, did so on the grounds that it lacked the crucial property rights distinctive of a dominant class. Since property in the means of production officially belonged to the people, there was a clear limit to the amount that could be diverted to the bureaucracy's personal use, and even this had to be done surreptitiously. Furthermore, such privileges as existed were tied to the occupation of a particular office, and were lost once the office was surrendered; above all, the bureaucracy's positions could not be transmitted to its children, so that it lacked the intergenerational continuity characteristic of a dominant class. It was unclear, moreover, where the boundaries of the class were to be drawn. If it included all officials, it was enormous, comprising technical strata, intellectuals, industrial managers, who had very different interests from the central bureaucracy. If it was more limited, it was not evident at what point or on what principle the limit should be drawn. Altogether, the bureaucracy lacked the coherence and solidity which a dominant class obtains from its distinctive principle of property ownership; it had no legitimacy or historical function separate from the revolution and its socialized property. As a consequence, it was vulnerable in a way a dominant class was not to a process of non-revolutionary political change, whereby the working class could come to regain control over what was publicly admitted to be its own, without any transformation in the system of law or property rights. And it was in virtue of this already socialized system of property that the USSR deserved support against Western capitalism.

In answer to these arguments, those who held that the bureaucracy constituted a dominant or ruling class did so on the grounds

that the crucial power which property ownership conveys is the
control over the surplus product, and the process of its extraction.
This the bureaucracy enjoyed through its monopoly of political and
administrative power. To say that this power was merely political
was to overlook the economic significance of administrative or
political positions within a state-owned property system, and the
varying role that the political domain has played in different
historical modes of surplus extraction. From the standpoint of the
direct producers, it was irrelevant how much or little of this surplus
was diverted by the exploiting class to its own personal use, if they
themselves exercised no control over it whatsoever, i.e., if the
product of their own labour confronted them as an alien power. In
any case, the privileges of bureaucrats and party officials were not to
be underestimated, nor their ability to use their office and contacts
to secure favourable opportunities for their children. But the
cohesion of this class was not secured intergenerationally, as in a
system of private property, but through the institution of the party,
and its 'nomenklatura' system. It was this institutional cohesion that
would necessitate a new revolutionary movement to displace the
bureaucracy. And as a system of class exploitation, there was no
ground in principle for preferring the USSR to Western capitalism;
it could only be a matter of particular policies, which might merit
defence.

Yet what of the argument, first advanced by Trotsky himself, that
the bureaucracy could not constitute a class because it had no
historical function? Here defenders of the ruling class theory
diverged considerably. On the one side were new class theorists
such as Burnham, who based their argument for the domination of
bureaucracy on the essential role played by its technical and
organizational skills in an advanced system of production. This
delivered the pessimistic, Weberian conclusion that the proletariat
was incapable of ever controlling its own destiny. At most there
could be intra-class conflicts, between central bureaucrats and
industrial managers or technical intelligentsia, who might appeal to
the working class for support. On the other side were writers such as
more recently Rudolph Bahro (*The Alternative in Eastern Europe*),
who argued that the bureaucracy performed the crucial historical
function, equivalent to the capitalists in the West, of ensuring the
enforced accumulation necessary to industrial take-off. On this
view, the bureaucracy was not, as the new class theorists asserted, a

post-capitalist class necessary to an advanced system of production. It was a substitute-capitalist class necessary to the process of industrialization in a society where capitalism was unable to perform this task for itself.

Bahro's argument was rooted firmly in a central idea of Marx's theory of history. This is that class exploitation is both necessary and historically progressive. Civilization could only have advanced at all by the forcible extraction of a surplus from the direct producers, which left a class free from manual labour to follow those political, scientific and cultural pursuits that the level of economic development could not make possible for all. By democratic process societies could never have advanced. In particular, the levels of surplus accumulation necessary for industrial take-off could never have been agreed democratically, since they involved the sacrifice of a generation to the future that no one would ever voluntarily accept. Class exploitation is thus both the price to be paid for economic underdevelopment, and the necessary condition for overcoming it.

But at the point when the work of primitive accumulation is accomplished, and the productivity of labour is well advanced through industrialization, at that point the exploiting class, capitalist or bureaucratic, becomes no longer historically necessary, since the level of economic and cultural development attainable by all allows for further social advance to be made by democratic agreement. Not only is the exploiting class unnecessary; it is socially regressive, since its power and privileges are no longer related to any justifiable function. At the same time, the energies of the population at large are directed from the creative role they could play in a democratically ordered social development, into resentment at their subordination, and the search for ways of subverting authority, or making its regime at least personally tolerable. The purpose of Bahro's work was to demonstrate for Soviet-type societies what Marx's had for capitalist ones: the point where the system, which had served the process of primitive accumulation, became increasingly destructive of social energies as economic development advanced, and it became ripe for replacement.

When the moment of replacement came, however, in the 'velvet revolutions' of 1989, the Communist system proved much more vulnerable to internal pressure than its capitalist counterpart, and in a different direction from that expected by its Marxist critics: not

onwards towards a reformed and democratized type of socialism,
but backwards towards capitalism. Once invited to make a choice,
the citizens of the former Communist countries found the prospects
of an untried third way between the command economy and free-
market capitalism insufficiently attractive. The fact that in the transition to capitalism many bureaucrats continued to enjoy a privileged existence, either through the continuity of the state
administration, or by using their personal networks to transform
themselves into entrepreneurs, was less important than that the
monolithic grip of the party bureaucracy over civil life was decis-
ively broken through a combination of electoral competition and
the reintroduction of private property in the means of production.

Many Marxists would, however, contest the prevalent view that
the lesson to be drawn from the demise of Communism and the
return to capitalist 'normalcy' is that any socialist alternative must
be economically unworkable and politically oppressive. The lesson
they would draw is a different one: trying to run a command
economy from a single centre without effective democratic accountability will result in a new exploiting class, based upon its monopoly
of administrative control over public property on one side and the
continued subordination of labour on the other. According to this
view the end of class society can only come when the class-forming
powers of private property over the means of production *and* the
powers of monopoly over administration of the productive process
alike are ended. Institutionally, this requirement could be met by a
system of social ownership within a market economy, in which
productive units were directly accountable to their own workforce,
as well as government being democratically accountable to its
citizens at the centre. Only in such a post-class society could
administration in economy and state lose its distinctive *bureaucratic*
character, as an instrument for social control.

Beyond bureaucracy?

From both the Weberian and Marxist accounts considered it should
be evident that there are two different dimensions to any theory of
bureaucratic power. One is the explanation for that power, and the
way it is organized, in terms of the social function bureaucracy
serves. As we have seen, the Marxist theory explains bureaucratic
power in terms of its class regulating function, rather than simply its

organizational function within industrial society, and consequently holds out the prospect of a non-bureaucratic form of administration in a socialist order beyond class divisions. The second dimension concerns the social force which the theory counterposes to bureaucracy as a means for holding it in check. In the Weberian theory this consists in the power of the individual leader, as validated in the process of industrial and electoral competition. In the Marxist theory it consists in the force of a proletarian democracy. Trotsky's account of the rise of the bureaucracy in the USSR traced the way that administrative power within both party and state increased in step with the decline in the vigour of proletarian democracy. The strengths of the two were inversely related. By the same token, the possibility of a non-bureaucratic administration in a society beyond classes would be systematically related to the vigour of its democratic life.

What form might such a democracy take, and what type of administration would it require? Marxists have always been notoriously reluctant to draw up blueprints for a socialist society, on the grounds that only a future generation will know what problems it has to solve. Yet some conception of an alternative society is implicit in any critique of the present, and is needed to justify any attempt to transform it. Such discussions as there are within Marxism about the shape of socialist administration tend to proceed in one of two directions, both of which can be traced back to Marx himself. The first sees a democracy of producers as incompatible with any hierarchy or specialist division of labour, which assigns different roles to individuals permanently, on a lifelong basis. Such specialization, it is argued, will give rise to an élite corps, which raises itself above the people; and in any case it contradicts the ideal of the all-round individual, transcending the division between manual and intellectual labour. Administration in a socialist society should either be shared by all as part of their civic responsibility ('everyone their own bureaucrat'), or be performed on the basis of rotation ('back to the masses').

The second tendency argues that a radical elimination of the division of labour is incompatible with the nature of advanced industrial production, and would undermine the levels of productivity necessary to a society without class antagonism, and to an active participatory democracy. A socially owned enterprise, in which policy was made by a workers' council, with representation from the wider community, would need a staff of experts to advise on policy, and a structure of trained administrators to coordinate its execution. How would this differ from a Weberian bureaucracy? Some features – clearly defined competence, rule-governed operation – would of course be the same. But equally an administrative system in which those subordinate to its authority also shared in determining its policy would be very different from one where they had no such role. The work discipline would not be an externally imposed one; there would be no point in secrecy or the monopolization of information; it would be difficult for permanent status differences to develop, since the subordinate would also share in governing the enterprise, either directly or through elected representatives.

If the earlier writings of Marx and Engels inclined towards the first of the above positions, their later writings tended towards the second. This was partly the result of a more realistic appreciation of the specialist technical and administrative requirements of the modern enterprise. It was also the result of developing a sharper differentiation between two senses of the division of labour, the technical and social respectively. The technical division of labour comprised those specialist functions that were intrinsic to industrial manufacture under any property system. The social division comprised those roles that were specific to the class society of capitalism. Prescriptions for a radical elimination of every division of labour failed to observe this distinction. However, it was also implicit in Marx's later thinking that, without an active democracy, the technical division could become the basis for a new social one. Hence the insistence in his writings on the Paris Commune that the administrative officers of a model commune should be paid a labourer's wages, and be strictly accountable to the people's representatives. At the same time any effective democracy would presuppose a universal system of education, extending far beyond the needs of particular work roles, which would itself erode the wider social consequences of the division between mental and manual labour. In effect Marx's solution to any inequalities inherent in the specialization and administrative hierarchy inseparable from industrial production was not the dismantling of the technical division of labour, but its transcendence by a system of democracy that would prevent it from consolidating into a new social division of classes.

The gulf between these expectations of Marx and the actual historical experience of societies governed in the name of Marxism-Leninism could hardly be wider. The explanation for this gulf in terms of the unfavourable circumstances and premature conditions in which its revolutions have taken place cannot be totally satisfactory, without a consideration of the Marxist theory and practice of democracy itself. The theory, despite its radically democratic intent, contains a number of flaws, which stem from Marx himself, but become exaggerated in the works of later Marxists.

We could distinguish at least three different limitations in the Marxist conception of democracy. First, for all that it advocates a rich democratic participation at grass-roots level (through communes, councils, soviets, and the like), it has never developed credible institutions for popular accountability at the governmental level, owing to its historic hostility to parliamentary representation as a bourgeois institution. This inadequacy has been the more damaging, the more functions a central government has been expected to undertake. The hostility towards parliamentarism has of course been linked to a suspicion of multi-party competition, and a refusal to share power over time with those whose commitment to a socialist transformation was suspect, or who might promote a return to capitalism. Whether such exclusivity is intrinsic to any serious socialist project is a matter of debate, but it is particularly evident in Marxism.

This exclusivity has been reinforced, secondly, by a privileging of the proletariat over other social classes, and of class over other forms of social subordination. This follows from Marxism's assumption that the working class has the strongest interest in a classless society, and that its voice must therefore be privileged over others in a democracy, especially one engaged in a transition to socialism. The historical record suggests, however, that where a democracy is based, not upon a robust defence of individual civil and political rights for all, but on its instrumental value to some future goal, the rights of the working class themselves become vulnerable to erosion, even where it constitutes a majority of the population.

Third, for all Marxism's insistence on popular control from below, it has also from the outset evidenced a markedly scientistic tendency, in its assumption that the course of history can be objectively known. From this it follows that identifying the right course of public policy is more a matter of discovering the truth by those with adequate training, than of ascertaining what the people, freely organized, will accept. Any theory which holds that the social good can be scientifically known will end up with an élitist form of decision making, however much it may espouse democracy in principle.

What has all this to do with bureaucracy? If the Marxist theory is correct in asserting that the power of bureaucracy is inversely proportionate to the strength of democracy, then the theoretical foundation and practical institutions of that democracy as well as the human material available for it must be a matter of critical concern. And especially so where the theory of democracy itself contains the seeds of its own degeneration in a bureaucratic direction. To the extent that this is so, the inadequacy of the Marxist theory of proletarian democracy also reveals the limitations of its analysis of bureaucratic power, and points beyond a theory that can be couched in purely Marxist terms.

Conclusion

This survey of the Weberian and Marxist analyses of bureaucracy has provided us with the materials both for a critique of each, and for the development of a theory of bureaucratic power that draws on the strengths of both. The starting point must be with the assumption they both share: in contrast to the more limited perspectives discussed in Chapter 1, the key to understanding bureaucratic power lies in its location within wider social and historical processes, and in the social function that it performs. That location and that function together determine the structure of bureaucratic organization, and the character of bureaucratic ideology and interests. It is worth stressing that this assumption underpins Weberian as much as Marxist theory, contradicting those who persist in defining Weber as an individualist in his sociological method, rather than in his political convictions.

From this common starting point the two theories diverge. According to the Weberian analysis, bureaucracy is to be understood in the context of a theory of modernization, and in terms of its organizational function in a mass industrial society. Its structure derives on the one hand from basic principles of modern authority and technical rationality; on the other from the hierarchical requirements of coordinating the complex division of labour within economy and state. Together these produce an impressive organiz- ational capacity, which is the source of the power of bureaucracy as a social group. This power is legitimated both on the basis of its necessary social function, and through the wider authority of technical rationality and specialist expertise in modern life. These legitimations only remain valid, however, if the administrative and technical role of the bureaucracy is subordinated to the goal- directing, value-determining agency of leading individuals, and does not itself become dominant. Such dominance is threatened by the extensive concentration of a single bureaucracy across different sectors of social life, and by the absence or weakness of countervail- ing structures of economic and electoral competition, through which individual leaders emerge with the authority to govern.

The Marxist theory, it should be said at once, recognizes some of these features. In particular, it acknowledges the necessity of a technical division of labour in modern society, and a hierarchy of authority to coordinate it. But it is not this, in its view, that explains the power of bureaucracy, and the difficulty of controlling it. That is to be located, rather, in the class division of industrial and industrializing societies, and in the function of bureaucracy in directly controlling the extraction of a surplus product, and regulating class conflict; to analyse this requires a political economy of class, rather than a political sociology of organization. It is bureaucracy's social function, not its technical one, and the wider influences of a class society to which it is subject, that explain those elements in its structure and operation which make it so formidable. The problem of bureaucratic power is one of the *intensive* concen- tration of power necessary to secure the social control of labour, rather than the *extensive* spread of the administrative system as such. Bureaucratic ideologies legitimate this power by obscuring its class function behind claims to serve the general interest, the requirements of order, the demands of technical necessity or efficiency. At this point the Weberian theory, for all its critique of bureaucracy, itself aids the legitimation of bureaucracy by present- ing what are the requirements of a social or class division as if they were the product of a technical one, with the conclusion that the emancipation of labour from its subordinate position is an impossi- bility.

At first sight these theories are flatly contradictory. What we have to ask, however, is whether they are intrinsically so; or whether, as so often happens in the social sciences, they only become so by an elevation of a partial perspective into the whole truth. The answer is surely that the two analyses are complementary, rather than mutually exclusive, and that we should pay attention to what each affirms, rather than what it overlooks, or denies. Weberian political sociology identifies the organizational power of a professional administration, the dangers of its extensive concentration, and the possibility of technical rationality becoming supreme in a society governed by a scientific world view. But it is blind to the class dimension of bureaucracy's function in capitalist societies, and the intensive concentration of power that derives from this. Marxist political economy, for its part, makes the class-regulating dimension of bureaucracy central to its analysis, but seriously underestimates the danger of an extensive concentration of administrative power, when harnessed to the authority claims of specialist knowledge – claims to which the character of its own scientific theory favourably disposes it. For an adequate understanding of bureaucratic power, we have to combine both these dimensions. We need, that is to say, a theory of modern society as such, *and* of its class divisions; a political sociology of organization, as well as a political economy of class. Equipped with both we shall find, not surprisingly, that the factors contributing to the power of bureaucracy are multidimensional, rather than monocausal.

Both theories involve a selective perception, whose strength and limitation alike derive from the powerful focus of a particular social standpoint and its values: those of a liberal élitism and a proletarian socialism respectively. And the elevation of each theory into the whole truth, which renders them mutually exclusive, derives from the universalist claims associated with each position. Weberian theory, which locates the source of modern Western civilization in the power of individualism, sees non-bureaucratic élites as the exclusive bearers of this key value in a bureaucratic age. And the conditions for the flourishing of these élites, the competition of the economic and political marketplace, are also defined as the conditions for preserving freedom for all. The validity of such a linkage, however, remains dubious. The history of the twentieth century suggests that the circumstances when powerful leaders give decisive direction to the bureaucracy can also be those which most threaten a general liberty; and that the best guarantee of individual freedom lies not in the striving of individual élites, but in the collective defence of an active democracy. However, since such a democracy would threaten the decisional scope and economic privileges of élites, the connection between it and the defence of individual freedom has to be denied by Weberian theory, and democratic institutions made simply into a vehicle for the emergence and assertion of leadership.

Marxism for its part claims to represent, not the individualist values of the bourgeois era, but the collective values necessary to the future preservation and further development of industrial societies. As the bearer of these values, the proletariat embodies the future interests of society as a whole. In consequence, Marxism offers a much richer conception of democracy than the plebiscitary conception of Weberian theory. However, in restricting this democracy to the proletariat, and turning its back completely on liberalism's values – including those necessary to democracy itself, such as a concern with individual rights and limited power – while accepting only liberalism's material and scientific achievements, Marxism is unable to secure the social emancipation it promises, even for the proletariat. As with Weberian theory, the limitations of its standpoint prevent it from adequately grasping the problem of bureaucratic power, or providing a convincing solution to it.

It follows that only a democratic theory which is strong enough to incorporate liberal features without being subordinated to them can offer an adequate theoretical or practical solution to the issues of bureaucratic power. By the same token, only such a theory provides the standpoint from which it is possible to integrate the insights of Weberian political sociology and Marxist political economy into a satisfactory synthesis. To demonstrate this conclusion, and also to locate the concern of the first chapter with administrative efficiency in its rightful place, will be the task of the remaining part of the book.

Notes

1 M. Weber, *Economy and Society*, p. 223.
2 M. Weber, *Economy and Society*, p. 1403.
3 Quoted in D. Beetham, *Max Weber and the Theory of Modern Politics*, p. 81.
4 M. Weber, *Selections in Translation*, ed. W.G. Runciman, p. 260.
5 Quoted in L. Trotsky, *The Revolution Betrayed*, p. 56.
6 op. cit., p. 113.
7 op. cit., p. 89.

3

Bureaucracy and Democratic Theory

Introduction

The argument of this book is that the task of understanding bureaucracy can only be approached through the different theoretical and disciplinary perspectives within which the subject has been treated; and that to construct a conceptual map of definitions of bureaucracy is at the same time to chart the relationship between the social sciences themselves. It is not only a matter of disciplinary perspectives, however, but also of the practical and normative standpoints from which they perceive bureaucracy as significant, and define the issues of bureaucratic efficiency and bureaucratic power as problematical. The question now is how to achieve a critical synthesis of these perspectives, so as to reach a definitive understanding of the subject. This cannot be done by standing outside every tradition of academic enquiry or theoretical position; that can only produce an unsystematic eclecticism. The task demands a tradition and a standpoint that are strong enough to comprehend the others.

The academic tradition is provided by political philosophy, which offers a framework both for the critical analysis of values, and for the exploration of the social and institutional conditions necessary to their realization. We have seen that the historical sociologies of Weber and Marx make an important contribution to the latter enterprise, in their analyses of the conditions for realizing liberty and democracy respectively in industrialized societies. But for different reasons they offer little help towards the critical analysis of values: Marxism, because it subordinates such an analysis to its doctrine of historical evolution; Weberian theory, because it defines values as a matter of subjective affirmation rather than reasoned argument. It is from within a tradition of philosophical analysis that I wish to argue that only a democratic theory incorporating liberal principles can provide the standpoint from which to reach a definitive understanding of bureaucracy.

A convenient starting point is to ask the question: why is it that people dislike bureaucracy, and perceive it as undesirable? A simple answer is that they see its authority as an imposition, and a limitation on their autonomy. However, liberals and democrats tend to understand the concept of autonomy differently. Liberals define autonomy as freedom of individual choice, which bureaucracy restricts; to bureaucracy they counterpose the market, as the sphere of individual choice and voluntary exchange, whose scope they seek to protect and expand. Democrats define autonomy as taking part in determining the rules and policies of the collective life; to them bureaucracy appears as an imposed or alien authority which they have had no share in, and in relation to which they seek to expand the sphere of democratic decision and control. From these contrasting conceptions of autonomy derive two familiar antitheses: bureaucracy vs. the market, and bureaucracy vs. democracy. And with each come two competing strategies when bureaucracy bulks large, or seems especially burdensome: expand the sphere of individual choice; extend the scope of democratic decision and control.

Now it should readily be apparent that these are not mutually exclusive strategies or antitheses. Those who pose the alternative bureaucracy or market are concerned with the respective scope of two different principles or spheres of social coordination – political authority and voluntary exchange respectively – and with where the line should be drawn *between* them. Those who pose the alternative bureaucracy or democracy are concerned with the sphere of political authority itself, and with how authority should be distributed and exercised *within* it. As the oversimplified diagram on p. 88 demonstrates, there are indeed two separate questions here. But they only appear mutually exclusive because the dichotomy bureaucracy or market makes the sphere of political authority coterminous with bureaucracy, so that the possibility of expanding the scope of democratic decision disappears from view; while the dichotomy bureaucracy or democracy tends to overlook, though it

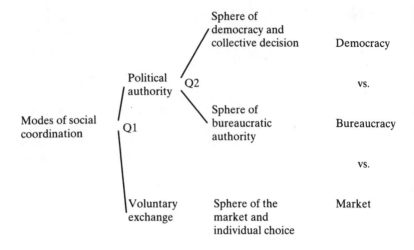

Q1 What should be the respective scope of political authority and
    voluntary exchange?
Q2 What should be the respective scope of democratic decision and
    bureaucratic authority?

does not in principle exclude, the issue of the scope of political
authority as such. There is every reason, however, why we should
be concerned with autonomy both as individual choice and as the
right to share in collective decisions; with the problems raised by the
expansion of the sphere of political authority, as well as with the
way that authority is distributed and arranged.

Nevertheless, determined protagonists of the market would
argue that the first question is the logically prior one, and that it is
appropriate to pose it in terms of the alternative bureaucracy or
market, for two reasons. First, the larger the scope of political
authority, the more difficult it is to subject it to democratic decision
or control. The answer to the second question above is therefore
dependent upon the first; the distribution and arrangement of
political authority is determined by its extent. Moreover, since it is
popular pressure that is the main reason for the expansion of the
political sphere, democracy has a self-destructive tendency, which
can only be prevented by the most forthright defence of the sphere
of individual choice against the demands for such expansion

encouraged by electoral auctioneering. Secondly, the democratic process is a much less adequate method for satisfying people's wants than the market, since there will always be a dissatisfied minority who have the majority's wishes imposed upon them. The market will always satisfy a minority taste for, say, the purchase of a particular type of footwear. A decision on shoe production made by political authority, in contrast, however democratic, will leave such minorities unaccounted for. For both these reasons, therefore, the antithesis democracy or bureaucracy is misconceived. Democracy itself contributes to bureaucratic imposition, both through its pressures for expansion of the political sphere, and through the compulsion it exercises over minorities.

Defenders of democracy counter this argument by focusing on the inadequacies of the market as a protector of autonomy. In the first place, they argue, the resources that different people bring to the market are unequal, and the character of markets is to intensify, rather than moderate, these inequalities. Left to themselves, markets will ensure freedom of choice for some while denying such freedom to others. Secondly, markets do not just consist of individuals, but of firms, i.e. bureaucratic hierarchies, to whose authority the majority of people are compelled to submit because they do not own any means of production of their own. In respect of both senses of autonomy, therefore, markets are found seriously wanting. And it is precisely their deficiencies that generate demands for expanding the sphere of political authority by way of compensation. In other words, calls to free the market in the face of bureaucracy are themselves self-contradictory, because they fail to recognize the powerful pressures for political expansion which the free market itself generates – pressures that can be suppressed for a time, but only by a highly coercive regime. The real problem of bureaucracy lies in the fact that these pressures take the form simply of passive demands for provision from the state, rather than of an active involvement of people in influencing the character of that provision, such as a more forthright interpretation of the 'democracy or bureaucracy' alternative would require.

There is a more powerful consideration than this, however, for regarding the issue of democracy, and of the distribution of political authority, as the prior one, and that is the simple point that the question of the scope of the market is itself properly the subject of political determination. This is not only a matter of historical fact, in that the market is as much a conscious political creation as the result of a process of quasi-natural evolution. It is also a matter of logic, in that the question of the scope of the political sphere must itself be among the most important questions for political authority to decide. Who should decide, and what should be the character of its authority, is therefore the basic question of political philosophy. And if we are concerned with the principle of equal right to autonomy, then the answer to that question can only be: a democratic authority. It is, after all, a strange concept of autonomy which accords people the right to decide what kind of shoes to buy, but allows them no part in deciding what kinds of choices should in principle be available in their society, within what limits, and how they should be distributed, i.e. no say in what kind of society they should live in. How this principle of autonomy can be realized in practice, and without self-contradiction, is the central problem of democratic theory.

It is a relatively simple matter to specify the basic principle of democracy as the equal right to share in deciding the rules and policies of the association of which one is a member, and to define the freedoms that are entailed by this principle: of thought, expression, association, assembly, and so on. It is much more difficult to determine how far it can be realized in practice, under what conditions, in a manner that is not self-contradictory. However, the agenda of problems involved will typically include the issues of bureaucracy considered so far in this volume. Where is the line between policy and administration to be drawn, and what is the relation between them? What is the meaning of administrative efficiency, how can it be attained, and to what extent is it advanced or hindered by the application of democratic principles? These are questions raised by the first chapter. What are the sources of bureaucratic power, under what circumstances may democracy itself contribute to its expansion, and what form should democratic institutions and practice take to control it? These issues were raised in the second chapter. In other words, the problems of democracy in the contemporary world, and those posed by bureaucracy are closely related. It is for this reason that the standpoint of democratic theory is the appropriate one for reaching a definitive understanding of bureaucracy, rather than the standpoint of an individualism which treats the political sphere as largely residual to the market, and thus has little interest in problems of its organization.

In considering the relationship between democracy and bureaucracy, however, we need to avoid the merely pejorative definitions of bureaucracy discussed in the Introduction, which deliver the conclusion that democracy and bureaucracy must be *intrinsically* contradictory: democracy, good; bureaucracy, bad. This common pejorative use will exclude any more complex analysis such as this book has so far suggested to be necessary. If bureaucracy is to be understood as the most general type of professional, rule-governed administration characteristic of modern industrial societies, we need to know, first, *what form* of this administration is compatible with democratic principles; and, secondly, *under what circumstances* the characteristics that make bureaucracy necessary may develop into an anti-democratic force. These questions will form the subjects of the following two sections.

Democracy and administrative efficiency

Intrinsic to the idea of democracy is a distinction between decisions of principle and priority in matters of policy and legislation, and the technical expertise which is necessary to reach a well-informed decision and to carrying it out effectively. If we examine the earliest Western democracy for which records exist, that of ancient Athens, we find that its citizens approved law and policy in person, through attendance at the assembly, and also took part in general administration on the basis of rotation. However, they made considerable use of technical experts, such as architects, naval designers, etc., both to advise on and to execute particular aspects of policy. The distinction between the expertise of these specialists, and the knowledge required for deciding on law and policy, was fundamental to justifications for democracy, and a major point of challenge by its critics. Were the ends of public life something all could comprehend, or were they the subject of specialist knowledge like the technical skills? The answer given to this epistemological question distinguished supporters of democracy from advocates of aristocracy or enlightened monarchy. Democracy's philosophical foundation lay in the proposition that the ability to entertain a conception of the good life, and to work it out in practice, was not a matter of technical knowledge, but could be attained by all, though as is well known women and slaves were excluded on the basis of arguments that have not stood the test of time.

The philosophical foundation of equal citizenship in the modern world is essentially the same as that of ancient Athens. But the roles of both policy making and legislation on one side and administration on the other have developed into full-time occupations, for reasons of both time and space. In an increasingly complex world citizens do not all have the necessary time to devote to politics or administration in person for their judgements to be sufficiently well-considered; and the scale of territory prevents them from all congregating together in one place (though modern means of communication are modifying this constraint). The spatial constraint, however, is not just a matter of physical congregation. On the one hand there is the need to simplify and crystallize the multiplicity of different viewpoints of a large society in a representative assembly, where policy differences can be focused and negotiated. Political parties have their rationale in this need also. On the other hand, there has to be a concentration of information and administrative capacities within a small enough compass for them to be readily brought to bear upon the formation and implementation of policy. And this can be most effectively done by those who have developed expertise in administration, both as a general activity and in particular areas of policy.

Now the ancient Athenian distinction between the evaluation and determination of ends, which all citizens are capable of, and the technical evaluation and determination of means, which is a matter for experts, is preserved in the modern democratic order in the division of roles between the politician and administrator respectively, and in two radically different forms of 'professionalization'. Politicians, as representatives, act simply in place of citizens, from whom they are differentiated, not by superior qualities or expertise, but only in the time their position allows them to devote to the activity. They take decisions on law and policy not in their own right, but on behalf of their constituents. Their capacity lies precisely in their representativeness, and the ultimate test of law and policy is its acceptability to those they represent. Hence derive elections as the method of appointment for democratic politicians, and the criteria of openness, responsiveness and accountability for the performance of their office.

The responsibility of administrators, on the other hand, lies in the quality of their professional service of advice and implementation. They are chosen not by election for their representativeness, but by appointment for their professional or technical skills. Their concern for policy is in the first instance with its feasibility – whether it can be implemented and how – more than its acceptability. But they take no responsibility for the policy itself; their responsibility is that of the subordinate, to accept what representatives decide or approve as their instruction.

It is a commonplace of policy analysis that this idealized distinction between politician and administrator, and the neat separation between ends and means on which it is based, tends to break down in practice, at a number of different points. And this is typically held to be damaging to the democratic theory from which the distinction derives. However, it is precisely at these points that democratic criteria can be brought into play, to help define a distinctively democratic form of administration.

A first point is one we have already encountered in Chapter 1. This is that policies are always a combination of ends and means, since technical considerations of feasibility, cost and impact on other policies all have an important bearing on the eventual choice and shape of a given policy. Such considerations are rarely uncontestable. Here is one point at which administrative officials can often come to determine policy choices through the selection of evidence that they present, thus *de facto* assuming the policy-making function. A democratic solution to this difficulty lies in two directions. One is that the politicians who have the formal responsibility for policy should have systematic avenues through which a range of technical evidence is available to them, either through the civil service itself, or through access to alternative sources of expertise. As the anarchist Bakunin is said to have remarked, the only external authority he recognized beyond his own conscience was that of the expert, but even then he would always consult two of them. From a democratic point of view, however, there is a further requirement: that the assumptions and considerations on which policy is based should also be open to public inspection, so that they can be tested in the wider context of an informed public opinion. There is nothing intrinsic to the activity of professional administration as such which requires it to be secretive, and every reason in a democratic order why it should not be, if political decision making is to be effectively accountable.

A second point where considerations of implementation typically come to determine policy outcomes is where their effectiveness depends upon the cooperation of powerful economic interests – business, professional, union or whatever – whose direct relationship with a bureaucracy can determine if not pre-empt the judgement of elected politicians. From one point of view direct consultation with freely organized interests is itself a feature of democratic policy making, and striking a sustainable compromise between them is part of the politician's distinctive function. Yet the normal bias of such consultation tends to favour intense and well-organized minorities, especially where these have developed long-term relations with, and privileged access to, a department of state and its civil servants, or enjoy a dominant position on its advisory panels. Democratizing the process of consultation would require that all relevant interests should have a formalized right of access to administrators in the preparation of policy, with publicly available minutes of proceedings, so that the weight given to them in policy decisions would be transparent and subject to publicly defensible justification.

A third point at which the distinction between ends and means breaks down is in the way that the character of policy can be affected by the manner of its implementation in practice. Lack of clarity in policy goals may leave considerable scope to administrators over their interpretation. Or the allocation of inadequate resources may require that decisions on priorities have to be made at the stage of implementation. Or the policy itself may intentionally leave considerable room for administrative discretion. It is precisely such areas of discretion that offer an opportunity for citizen involvement, especially in the delivery of public services. This could take the form, as appropriate, of service decentralization to the neighbourhood level; of elected representation on local management boards; of opinion surveys and citizen panels to help determine local priorities and appropriate performance criteria in service provision; and so on. Although such forms of citizen involvement would not rule out individual redress in the event of inadequate performance or maladministration (e.g. through an Ombudsman or customer's charter), they offer a different model for administrative responsiveness from that of the market: collective negotiation in advance, rather than individual 'exit' after the event.

What these examples indicate is that it is not the absence of a professionalized bureaucracy that characterizes a democratic system of administration, but the cultural values and norms by which such a bureaucracy operates: plurality and openness of professional advice; equity and transparency in access to consultation; responsiveness to citizens in service delivery. In view of the complexity of the relation between ends and means in policy decision and implementation, these democratic criteria have to permeate the administrative system as well as the political process itself. But there is nothing about them which is *inherently* contradictory to the features which Weber defined as essential to bureaucracy, as a glance back at the list on pp. 9–10 will show. It is often said, for example, that the concept of a profession itself presupposes superior knowledge exercised paternalistically within a closed system of self-regulation. But that is itself a cultural manifestation, typical of precisely those professions that are least accountable to those they serve, and not intrinsic to the exercise of technical skill as such. What is distinctive of a democratic administration is that the bureaucratic principle of accountability upwards of each administrator to a superior is complemented by the accountability of the administrative system as a whole to the public at large.

But are these democratic criteria compatible with administrative efficiency? Openness, consultation, responsiveness always seem more time-consuming, and therefore, expensive, from a short-term point of view. In the longer term, however, such criteria constitute an important discipline for an administrative system in the public domain that is not subject to market competition: to minimize maladministration; to expose corruption; and to prevent the adoption or continuation of wasteful or unworkable policies. A similar conclusion is suggested if we broaden our concept of efficiency from narrow cost-efficiency to the wider effectiveness of policies. As we saw in Chapter 1, there is no single criterion such as profitability to assess the effectiveness of policies in the public sector; effectiveness is a matter of finding a balance between competing values that is publicly justifiable and acceptable, and can be seen to work in practice. Here the form of administration has its own contribution to make to the broader democratic principle of government by consent.

In assessing the contribution of the administrative system itself to the realization of this principle, however, it is important not to assign to it responsibility for defects which may belong to the wider political system. Because bureaucracy is omnipresent, forming the point at which people experience government directly, most problems are transmitted through it, and become perceived as problems *of* bureaucracy, though their source may lie elsewhere. In this sense bureaucrats are the 'flakcatchers' for every failing of the democratic order. Thus, for example, many of the features which give people a sense of powerlessness in relation to government are to be located in the representative process itself: its remoteness, lack of effective accountability, inadequate representativeness, and so on. Complaints about bureaucracy may be a convenient way for politicians to deflect attention from their own failings, but do not necessarily assist accurate analysis.

The same point can be made about the wider political and social processes which may contribute, under given conditions, to bureaucracy becoming an anti-democratic force. The argument of this section, it should be clear, is that, although bureaucracy embodies features such as a concentration of information and organizational capacity, which have the potential for being used anti-democratically, these are not anti-democratic in themselves, but are necessary to the administrative requirements of a democratic order. Those who do not acknowledge this, but hold that democracy and bureaucracy are inherently contradictory, tend to be driven in one of two directions: to Utopianism or to pessimism. To Utopianism, on the part of those who see no prospect for a democratic order other than to abandon professional administration altogether. To pessimism, on the part of those who accept the necessity of professional administration, but therefore see democracy as irretrievably compromised by an anti-democratic power at its heart. Neither is able to pose the question correctly: under what circumstances does bureaucracy become self-enclosed and secretive, and its organizational power come to serve a controlling and manipulative purpose? These will be explored in the following section.

Democracy and bureaucratic power

The conclusion reached from the analysis of theories of bureaucratic power in Chapter 2 was that the pressures which push bureaucracy in an anti-democratic direction do not derive autonomously from within the administrative system, but are the result of the kind of tasks it is required to accomplish. It is no use therefore blaming the bureaucracy for causes which lie outside itself. Secrecy, for example, only becomes endemic because there are powerful reasons for hiding things from people on a continuing basis, other than simply the convenience of concealing the administration's own errors. If we look for the reasons, we shall find that they mostly have their origin in the need for the systematic control of social behaviour, in the absence of explicit consent to authority or policy. Although control and regulation are inseparable from any authority, it is possible to distinguish three major processes that can lead this control in the direction of bureaucratic independence and self-enclosure. The first is the management of unresolved social conflict. The second is the dynamic of the overextended centre. The third is the protection of the state's security interests. The first two processes are internal to the society, and are identified in the Marxist and liberal accounts considered in the previous chapter. The third derives from the situation of the state in the international order, and has not so far been mentioned. I shall consider each of the three briefly in turn.

As we saw in the previous chapter, the idea that the control of labour requires a secretive, self-enclosed administration is central to the Marxist theory of bureaucracy, in both industry and state. We do not have to accept the labour theory of value to recognize that minority control over the collective process and product of labour, whether under the rubric of private or public ownership, constitutes a major source of compulsion and social conflict in industrial societies. The fact of labour's subordination at the point of production, and the ceaseless change in the conditions of wage labour, make any concordat struck at the wider political level fragile and impermanent, in the absence of democratization at the level of the work place itself. However, there is a tendency within Marxism to underemphasize other independent sources of social control and conflict, whether involving other classes, or other dimensions of stratification, such as race, ethnicity or gender. Although these follow a different dynamic from the relationship of dominance and subordination constituted in the process of production, nevertheless, to the extent that any subordinate group has to be controlled or managed through administrative means, in the absence of genuine social agreement, bureaucracy will develop a protective cloak of secrecy in order to carry out its function, whether in the interests of 'efficiency' or 'order'.

The dynamic of the overextended centre follows a different logic, since the need for social control arises as a byproduct of the overextension of the state itself, in pursuit of other goals. The most considered analysis derives from the liberal critique of the command economy, and its contention that if political authority is required to bear too much of the weight of social coordination, in comparison with voluntary exchange, it becomes locked into a cycle of increasing compulsion. A similar point is made by critics of the overcentralized state, in its appropriation of all powers from independent local centres of political authority. Such a critique does not necessarily imply a rejection of central planning, in the sense of setting the framework for social and economic activity, or even of selective interventions within it, especially of a facilitative kind. What it asserts is that the more activities the centre seeks to control, the more the initiatives arising from society and the locality have to be stifled; at the same time the centre is unable to cope with the unintended consequences of its own interventions, and therefore seeks to take the activities over and make them the subject of its own administration. It thus becomes locked into a cycle of increasing interventions to correct the consequences of earlier ones. In this case the transformation of administration into an autonomous power takes place under a paternalist rubric: 'we can see the whole picture, and we know best'.

The third major cause of bureaucratic self-enclosure lies in the state's own security interests, and is sustained under the rubric of 'national security'. So far in this volume I have made little mention of the most basic historical rationale for state institutions: the maintenance of control over a given territory against external challenge. Of all functions this is the one most conducive to secrecy and the development of autonomy on the part of the state apparatus. Foreign policy is the least amenable of policy areas to democratic control; the information on which it is based cannot be tested against people's own experience, and their opinions are thus particularly subject to manipulation. Military security in face of potential enemies necessarily has its counterpart in secrecy in face of the home community, and the network of secrecy extends to the weapons industries, whose interests are closely entwined with those of the bureaucracy. Of course the degree of bureaucratic self-enclosure is partly dependent upon the extent of any external threat, and how far it is replicated internally. But it is also a matter of the state's own political posture and mode of defence. A great power role, or pretensions to it, is the posture most conducive to the expansion of the military related bureaucracy within the state, and to its infecting other areas of the apparatus; reliance on nuclear weapons systems leads to the most intense and ramified secrecy. At the other end of the spectrum, a posture of neutrality, protected by conventional defence and a citizen militia, is most conducive to limiting secrecy, and to containing its effects upon the administrative apparatus as a whole.

Common to all these three processes – the regulation of social subordination and conflict, the dynamic of the overextended centre, the protection of state security – is the need to control a population, or significant sections of it: to treat them as the objects of management, with all the sophisticated techniques that now implies, rather than as the autonomous subjects of social and political activity. To this end secrecy is required, and the informational and organizational capacities necessary to modern administration have to be transformed into an instrument of control and surveillance, and protected by a process of bureaucratic self-enclosure and independence. But if self-enclosure is necessary to protect bureaucracy from exposure to the population at large, to a certain extent it becomes protected from the policy makers also. Under this protection, the bureaucracy's own interests come to assume a special place in the formation of policy, and the values of administrative feasibility and technical rationality turn into ends in themselves, whether under the rubric of efficiency and order, of centralized planning, or the needs of state security. In other words, the theories of bureaucratic policy considered towards the end of Chapter 1 can now be seen as the characteristic product of bureaucratic self-enclosure. That self-enclosure creates the illusion that bureaucracy is an entirely autonomous and self-determining agency, rather than itself shaped by the social functions and processes which render that independence necessary.

Where Marxism tends to regard the processes of overcentralization and state security management as ultimately derivative from that of class conflict, I would argue that these constitute three independent sources of bureaucratic self-enclosure and autonomization. The degree to which this effect occurs depends upon the intensity of the processes, and on how far they overlap or reinforce one another, though of course considerations of political tradition and culture also play their part. In a society whose system of production requires intensified labour extraction, and where it meets with sustained resistance, the management of this process alone may be sufficient to propel the bureaucracy beyond any popular control, in state as well as economy. This is one typical source of dictatorship in the contemporary world. In the case of the USSR during the 1920s and 1930s, by contrast, we find the conjunction of all three processes, albeit following a different temporal dynamic: the assertion of state security interests against external and internal challenge; the overextension of the centre in the service of the command economy; the compulsory extraction of a surplus from both peasantry and proletariat in the interests of rapid industrial development. All this took place within a state tradition that had never experienced any liberal, let alone democratic, evolution. The development of bureaucracy into a self-enclosed, autonomous power, was thus heavily overdetermined.

In the Western liberal democracies since 1945, these processes have generally been less acute, and have taken place within a political order already considerably democratized, though to a different extent in different countries. The necessity of social control, however, whether deriving from unresolved social conflict, or overextension of the centre, or state security interests, exerts a continuous pressure for secrecy, though within a relatively open democratic culture. We thus find a conjunction of contradictory elements within the state bureaucracy, which combines the characteristics of a publicly accountable administration with tendencies towards bureaucratic self-enclosure and autonomy. This contradiction, which is naturally more acute in some agencies than others, is experienced as a conflict of responsibility on the part of civil servants, between answerability to their superiors and commitment to the norms of democratic accountability. Its most paradoxical manifestation is the conjunction of the 'official secret' with the 'unofficial leak': the officially approved attempt to conceal from parliament and the public what is immediately leaked with a good conscience by someone lower down. Civil servants are thus caught between conflicting demands: between the norms of democratic accountability on the one hand, and functions that require secrecy in the interests of effective political management on the other.

These contradictions take a particularly acute form in Britain, which explains why demands for freedom of information, and for greater political control of the civil service, constitute such a recurrent feature of its political agenda. Openness is the keystone of democratic politics, but proposals to achieve it are likely to prove insufficient when they take no account of the pressures causing secretiveness in the first place. Otherwise they are fated to follow the usual course of commitments to open government by opposition parties, which are abandoned as soon as they rediscover in office the compelling reasons for secrecy. Of course there is an institutional dimension to this as well, in that in a parliamentary system such as Britain's, there is always a majority of Members of Parliament who have a stronger interest in keeping the government in office than in exposing its actions to public view. Like the civil servants themselves, members of governing parties are caught in a conflict between their obligations to the government and their commitment to effective accountability. At the root of this conflict, however, lie the systemic features that make secrecy an unavoidable part of state policy, which have a particular tenacity in Britain, with its persistently unresolved conflicts of class, race and religion, its overcentralized system of government, and its continuing great power pretensions and nuclear armoury, which the end of the Cold War has done little to diminish. Such an agenda of problems of political management makes secrecy a pervasive habit throughout its administration.

Failure to diagnose this problem correctly is responsible for one of the persistent stereotypes of British politics: the weak-willed minister as tool of an all-powerful civil service. Of course there is a problem of bureaucratic power and its political control; my whole argument is that the process of administrative self-enclosure creates problems for ministers as well as for their parliamentary scrutineers. But the solution which simply advocates the exercise of ministerial machismo – the contemporary version of Weberian charismatic authority – whether or not backed up by political advisers, provides no answer to the problem of ministerial collusion in secrecy, or to the pressures that render it necessary. Proposals for open government, going beyond the merely cosmetic, could only be effective as part of an agenda of addressing these pressures directly, on the part of a government with clear priorities and able to command sustained popular support.

My conclusion, then, about democracy and bureaucratic power can be simply stated. It is that bureaucratic administration is not inherently anti-democratic. Its organizational capacities only become so when protected by secrecy, and it attains an independence of its own. This autonomy, though real, creates the illusion that bureaucracy is self-activating, when the reasons for its self-enclosure lie outside itself, in the tasks it is required to perform, and the wider social and political agenda of which these are a part. Any analysis must start with these. If it does not, we shall fail to understand why bureaucracies can be so successful in resisting attempts to make them more open and accountable. We shall thereby attribute to them a power greater than they possess, and make our own contribution to perpetuating the myths of bureaucratic malevolence or bureaucratic invincibility.

Conclusion

The standpoint of democratic theory, and its postulate of a realizable democratic order, has enabled us to combine an understanding of bureaucratic administration from within, with a critical analysis of bureaucratic power from without, and to incorporate both the liberal critique of the overextension of political authority, and the Marxist critique of bureaucracy as an instrument of social subordination and control. In the process, this standpoint offers a solution to the problems raised at the outset of the work. As to the question of definition it confirms the concept of bureaucracy as specifying only the most general features of a rule-governed professional administration; and the study of bureaucracy as comprising the study of this general form together with its distinctive variants, of which a bureaucracy working within a democratic order is particularly significant. In relation to the question of administrative efficiency, it identifies the conditions under which the necessary bureaucratic roles of ensuring the feasibility of policy and its effective implementation can be carried out without allowing considerations of feasibility or efficiency to short-circuit the debate about ends, or the negotiation of competing social claims. And in relation to bureaucratic power, it clarifies the process whereby the information and organizational capacities intrinsic to bureaucracy turn into an anti-democratic force, through secrecy and self-enclosure, and the characteristic pressures which lead it in that direction. In sum, the standpoint offers us the most complete, and I would argue definitive, analysis of the subject.

A final question remains. One of the recurrent themes of the book has been the way that particular conceptions of bureaucracy are aligned with distinct social positions and practical interests, from which they derive their characteristic insights and limitations. The perspectives of the first chapter are largely those of bureaucracy itself, with which the disciplines are closely associated in their education of recruits for posts in management and administration. As such they share the limitations of its perspective, both in their tendency to understand it entirely from within, as a self-moving entity, and in their narrow disciplinary conception of social science, which reflects the specialist function of administration within the social division of labour. The perspectives of the second chapter are broader, involving the understanding of social and historical processes as a whole, that is necessary to the political projects of major social classes, bourgeois and proletariat respectively. From these class positions also derive their characteristic limitations, both in the analysis of bureaucracy itself, and in their conception of social science as the world view of a particular social class. To what social standpoint and practical interests, then, does the perspective of democratic theory belong? Or does the claim that it offers a definitive or comprehensive analysis of bureaucracy involve the implausible supposition that it is detached from any social location whatsoever?

This question touches on one of the most fundamental issues of social theory. From the earliest period in the development of social science, it was recognized that the way society was perceived depended on the social location of the viewer; and that attempts to escape this social determination of knowledge by methodological means – e.g. by specifying a rigorous procedure of enquiry combined with an attitude of scientific detachment – could not overcome the problem of initial assumptions, or criteria of significance, which could only be socially derived. Since the problem was first posed, there have been broadly two responses to it. One has been to argue that a particular social position offers a privileged access to truth, because its outlook and interests represent the universal interests of society as a whole, and therefore its intellectual spokespeople can attain a universally valid knowledge. Various candidates for this privileged position have been suggested at different times, and for different reasons, including the bourgeoisie, the proletariat and the bureaucracy itself. As each of these claims has in turn been exposed as special pleading on behalf of a sectional group, however progressive, a second response has tended to become prevalent. This involves relativism in one form or another: either accepting that initial assumptions are socially dependent, that there is no agreed academic criterion for deciding between them, and that therefore it is a matter of political choice; or, alternatively, treating competing social theories simply as analytical tool-kits which will provide better explanations for some kinds of phenomena than others. Although the latter position may appear to escape the problem of social determination, it does so at the expense of surrendering any coherent agenda of its own, and accepting uncritically the agenda set by others.

The assumption underlying this book is that we should not give up the search for a comprehensive and coherent understanding of social processes – what used to be called the search for truth – which lies beyond the particularism of special disciplines, the competing world views of major social groups, and the eclecticism of 'multiple viewpoints'. And if we ask to whose perspective and practical requirements such a comprehensive understanding corresponds, the answer can only be: that of the democratic citizen. By 'democratic citizen' I do not mean those who happen to live in what we call a democracy. I mean anyone who is committed to the equality of democratic rights and to the resolution of differences by means of open discussion and negotiation, and who accepts the practice which these commitments entail. This position is a genuinely universal one, both in the sense that it is in principle open to all, and that it transcends the particular differences of social and personal identity, without abolishing them, or imagining them away. It alone as a form of social practice shares the same requirements as social science itself: the demand for openness of social institutions and activities, rather than their mystification through concealment or distortion of the truth; the necessity to understand the viewpoint and interests of those who differ from ourselves, i.e. to treat them as subjects rather than objects; finally, the need to comprehend social processes as a whole, as a condition for the establishment and maintenance of its own practice. Such requirements do not entail accepting all positions or interests as of equal worth. The standpoint of democratic citizenship is a critical one, especially of power roles whose exercise depends upon the systematic concealment and distortion of the truth, and the suppression of the claims of others. It is also revisionary, in that it seeks to expand the possession and exercise of democratic rights.

Such a standpoint does not of itself, of course, guarantee valid knowledge of society, in the absence of adequate methods of investigation. But it is the one most conducive to attaining it, and it therefore has a special significance for the practice of social science. By the same token, the general understanding of social processes that social science offers is of particular importance to the practice of democratic citizenship. It is not some lofty pinnacle to be attained by a special few, who are destined to become the philosopher supremos of the political order; nor yet a series of lesser peaks which form the preserve of bureaucratic and non-bureaucratic élites. It is a broad plateau, whose ascent should in principle be open to all who seek the exercise of democratic citizenship.

Bureaucracy is one of the most pervasive institutions of the modern world. The very familiarity of its presence obscures its complexity. As democratic citizens we need to understand both the value and the limits of its capacities, and the reasons why these become transformed into an independent power, if we are to extend the field of democratic practice itself. Whether this standpoint can indeed deliver the definitive analysis of bureaucracy that I boldly claim for it, is for you, the reader, to judge.

Further Reading

Full publication details are given in the Bibliography

Introduction

The problem of defining bureaucracy is discussed extensively in Albrow, and also in Bendix, Crozier (ch. 7), Jacques (ch. 3), Kamenka and Krygier (eds) (ch. 1), Lane (ed.) (ch. 1).

Chapter 1

Among the numerous approaches to bureaucracy from the standpoint of the sociology of organization are Blau and Meyer, Burns and Stalker, Clegg and Dunkerley, Gross and Etzioni, Merton (ed.), Mouzelis, Perrow and Woodward. Works devoted to various aspects of an economic or public choice approach are Breton and Wintrobe, Coase, Downs, Jackson, Marris, von Mises (1944), Niskanen (1971, 1973), Rowley (ed.) and Williamson. Useful summaries of the public choice approach are to be found in Moe (1984), Orzechowski, and criticisms of it in Dunleavy, Lewin and Self (1993). For public administration from a comparative point of view see Dunsire (1973), Nadel and Rourke, Page, Peters (1995), Piekalkiewicz and Hamilton, Riggs, Self (1972) and Subramaniam. For the distinction between public and private management see Allison, Moe (1990) and Ranson and Stewart. Niskanen's theory of budget maximizing is evaluated in Blais and Dion, Conybeare, Miller and Moe, and Wade. For a more complex account of government growth see Rose. Theories of bureaucratic competition are discussed in Jenkins and Grey, and Peters (1995), while Allison and Halperin's concept of 'bureaucratic politics' is criticized in Caldwell and Freedman. Various models of politician-bureaucrat relations are reviewed in Page, Peters (1987), and L.B. Hill.

Chapter 2

For treatments of Weber's theory of bureaucracy in the broader context of his politics and political sociology see Beetham (1985, 1989), Bendix and Roth, Glassman and Murvar (eds), Lassman and Speirs, and Mommsen (1974, 1989). His theory of rationalization is discussed in Brubaker, Roth and Schluchter, and Schluchter (1981). For comparisons between Weber and Michels see Gouldner, Mommsen (1981) and Scaff. Aspects of Weber's theory are compared with Marx or Marxism by Cohen, Kamenka and Krygier, Loewith and Wright. More fully developed criticisms of state planning than Weber's are in Hayek (ed.) (1935, 1944) and von Mises (1936). For Marx see Draper (1977), Perez-Diaz, and Schluchter (1987). Marxist accounts of bureaucracy are provided by Baptista, Deutscher (1972), Hegedus, Lefort and Mandel (1973, 1992). Trotsky's theory is discussed by Deutscher (1963) and Knei-Paz. Subsequent debates about the Soviet bureaucracy as a ruling class are in Burnham, Djilas and Rizzi, and more recent discussions in Arato, Bahro, Feher, Mallet, Mandel (1979), Sawer and Sweezy. Marxist theories of a future democratic order are treated in Draper (1970), Levin, Lukes, Ollman, Pierson (1986), Polan and Rattansi. For discussions of market socialism in the light of the Soviet experience see Bardhan and Roemer (eds), Brus, Nove, Nuti and Pierson (1995). Assessments of Marxism since 1989 are to be found in Blackburn (ed.) and Callinicos.

Chapter 3

The antithesis between democracy and the market is discussed in Beetham (1993a), Elster and Lindblom. More general discussions of democratic theory are to be found in Arblaster, Beetham (1993b), Dahl (1989), Duncan (ed.), Finley and Held. On bureaucracy and democracy see Abrahamsson, Etzioni-Halevy, Gruber, Pollitt and Thompson (1983), and for the responsibility of the administrator in a democratic order, Chapman (ed.), Cooper and

Thompson (1980). Ways of democratizing administration are considered in Albo, Langille and Panitch (eds), Frug, M.J. Hill, Ranson and Stewart, and Stivers. For the complexities of policy implementation see Dunsire (1978) and Pressman and Wildavsky; for pressure groups and bureaucracy see Page and Peters (1977). Sources of bureaucratic secrecy are analysed in Harden and Lewis, Michael, Nelkin, Ponting, Robertson and Rule; Kaufman and Milward and Rainey caution against exaggerating bureaucracy's failings. On democratizing the representative system see Barber and Fishkin, and extending democracy to the economic sphere, Archer, Dahl (1985) and Pateman. For the relation between social science and social interests see Habermas.

Bibliography

Abrahamsson, B. (1977) *Bureaucracy or Participation*. London: Sage.

Albo, G., Langille, D. and Panitch, L. (eds) (1993) *A Different Kind of State? Popular Power and Democratic Administration*. Toronto: Oxford University Press.

Albrow, M.C. (1970) *Bureaucracy*. London: Pall Mall Press.

Allison, G.T. (1983) Public and private management: are they fundamentally alike in all unimportant respects? in J.L. Perry and K.L. Kramer (eds) *Public Management: Public and Private Perspectives*, pp. 72–92. Palo Alto, CA: Mayfield Publishing.

Allison, G.T. and Halperin, M.H. (1972) Bureaucratic politics: a paradigm and some policy implications, in R. Tanter and R.H. Ullman (eds) *Theory and Policy in International Relations*, pp. 40–79. Princeton, NJ: Princeton University Press.

Arato, A. (1978) Understanding bureaucratic centralism. *Telos*, 35: 73–87.

Arblaster, A. (1994) *Democracy*, 2nd edn. Buckingham: Open University Press.

Archer, R. (1995) *Economic Democracy*. Oxford: Clarendon Press.

Bahro, R. (1978) *The Alternative in Eastern Europe*. London: New Left Books.

Baptista, J. (1974) Bureaucracy, political system and social dynamic. *Telos*, 22: 66–84.

Barber, B. (1984) *Strong Democracy*. Berkeley, CA: University of California Press.

Bardhan, P. and Roemer, J.E. (eds) (1993) *Market Socialism*. Oxford: Oxford University Press. 1993.

Beetham, D. (1985) *Max Weber and the Theory of Modern Politics*, 2nd edn. Cambridge: Polity Press.

Beetham, D. (1989) Max Weber and the liberal political tradition. *Archives Européennes de Sociologie*, 30: 311–23.

Beetham, D. (1993a) Four theorems about the market and democracy. *European Journal of Political Research*, 23: 187–201.

Beetham, D. (1993b) Liberal democracy and the limits of democratization, in D. Held (ed.) *Prospects for Democracy*, pp. 55–73. Cambridge: Polity Press.

Bendix, R. (1968) Bureaucracy, in the *International Encyclopaedia of the Social Sciences*, vol. II, pp. 206–19. New York: Macmillan and Free Press.

Bendix, R. and Roth, G. (1971) *Scholarship and Partisanship: Essays on Max Weber*. Berkeley, CA: University of California Press.

Blackburn, R. (ed.) (1991) *After the Fall*. London: Verso.

Blais, A. and Dion, S. (eds) (1991) *The Budget-maximizing Bureaucrat: Appraisals and Evidence*. Pittsburgh, PA: University of Pittsburgh Press.

Blau, P.M. and Meyer, M.W. (1971) *Bureaucracy in Modern Society*, 2nd edn. New York: Random House.

Breton, A. and Wintrobe, R. (1982) *The Logic of Bureaucratic Conduct*. Cambridge: Cambridge University Press.

Brubaker, R. (1984) *The Limits of Rationality*. London: Allen and Unwin.

Brus, W. (1972) *The Market in a Socialist Economy*. London: Routledge.

Burnham, J. (1945) *The Managerial Revolution*. Harmondsworth: Penguin Books.

Burns, T. and Stalker, G.M. (1961) *The Management of Innovation*. London: Tavistock Publications.

Caldwell, D. (1977) Bureaucratic foreign policy making. *American Behavioral Scientist*, 21: 87–110.

Callinicos, A. (1991) *The Revenge of History: Marxism and the East European Revolutions*. Cambridge: Polity Press.

Chapman, R.A. (ed.) (1993) *Ethics in Public Service*. Edinburgh: Edinburgh University Press.

Clegg, S. and Dunkerley, D. (1980) *Organization, Class and Control*. London: Routledge.

Coase, R. (1937) The nature of the firm. *Economica*, 4: 386–405.

Cohen, J.L. (1972) Max Weber and the dynamics of rationalized domination. *Telos*, 14: 63–86.

Conybeare, J.A.C. (1984) Bureaucracy, monopoly and competition. *American Journal of Political Science*, 28: 479–502.

Cooper, T.L. (1991) *An Ethic of Citizenship for Public Administration*. Englewood Cliffs, NJ: Prentice-Hall.

Crozier, M. (1971) *The Bureaucratic Phenomenon*. Chicago, IL: University of Chicago Press.

Dahl, R.A. (1985) *A Preface to Economic Democracy*. Cambridge: Polity Press.

Dahl, R.A. (1989) *Democracy and its Critics*. New Haven, CT: Yale University Press.

Deutscher, I. (1963) *The Prophet Outcast*. London: Oxford University Press.

Deutscher, I. (1972) The roots of bureaucracy, in I. Deutscher *Marxism in our Time*, pp. 181–208. London: Cape.

Djilas, M. (1957) *The New Class*. London: Thames and Hudson.

Downs, A. (1967) *Inside Bureaucracy*. Boston, MA: Little Brown.

Draper, H. (1970) The death of the state in Marx and Engels, in R. Miliband and J. Saville (eds) *Socialist Register*, pp. 281–308. London: Merlin Press.

Draper, H. (1977) *Karl Marx's Theory of Revolution*, vol. 1, *State and Bureaucracy*. New York: Monthly Review Press.

Duncan, G. (ed.) (1983) *Democratic Theory and Practice*. Cambridge: Cambridge University Press.

Dunleavy, P. (1991) *Democracy, Bureaucracy and Public Choice*. Hemel Hempstead: Harvester Wheatsheaf.

Dunsire, A. (1973) *Administration: the Word and the Science*. London: Martin Robertson.

Dunsire, A. (1978) *Implementation in a Bureaucracy*. Oxford: Martin Robertson.

Elster, J. (1986) The market and the forum, in J. Elster and A. Hylland (eds) *The Foundations of Social Theory*, pp. 103–32. Cambridge: Cambridge University Press.

Engels, F. (1959) On authority, in L. Feuer (ed.) *Marx and Engels*, pp. 418–4. New York: Basic Books.

Etzioni-Halevy, E. (1985) *Bureaucracy and Democracy*, 2nd edn. London: Routledge.

Feher, F., Heller, A. and Markus, G. (1983) *Dictatorship Over Needs*. Oxford: Blackwell.

Finley, M.I. (1973) *Democracy Ancient and Modern*. London: Chatto and Windus.

Fishkin, J. (1991) *Democracy and Deliberation*. New Haven, CT: Yale University Press.

Freedman, L. (1976) Logic, politics and foreign policy processes. *International Affairs*, 52: 434–49.

Frug, J. (1990) Administrative democracy. *University of Toronto Law Journal*, 40: 559–86.

Gerth, H.H. and Mills, C.W. (eds) (1948) *From Max Weber*. London: Routledge.

Glassman, R. and Murvar, V. (eds) (1984) *Max Weber's Political Sociology*. Westport, CT: Greenwood Press.

Gouldner, A. (1955) Metaphysical pathos and the theory of bureaucracy. *American Political Science Review*, 49: 496–507.

Gross, E. and Etzioni, A. (1985) *Organizations in Society*. Engle-wood Cliffs, NJ: Prentice-Hall.

Gruber, J.E. (1987) *Controlling Bureaucracies: Dilemmas in Democratic Governance*. Berkeley, CA: University of California Press.

Habermas, J. (1971) *Knowledge and Human Interests*. London: Heine-mann.

Harden, I. and Lewis, N. (1986) *The Noble Lie*. London: Hutchinson.

Hayek, F.A. (ed.) (1935) *Collectivist Economic Planning*. London: Routledge.

Hayek, F.A. (1944) *The Road to Serfdom*. London: Routledge.

Hegedus, A. (1976) *Socialism and Bureaucracy*. London: Allison and Busby.

Held, D. (1987) *Models of Democracy*. Cambridge: Polity Press.

Hill, L.B. (1991) Who governs the American administrative state? A bureaucratic-centred image of governance. *Journal of Public Administration Research and Theory*, 1: 261–94.

Hill, M.J. (1976) *The State, Administration and the Individual*. London: Fontana.

Jackson, P.M. (1982) *The Political Economy of Bureaucracy*. London: Philip Allan.

Jacques, E. (1976) *A General Theory of Bureaucracy*. London: Heine-mann.

Jenkins, W. and Gray, A. (1983) Bureaucratic politics and power: developments in the study of bureaucracy. *Political Studies*, 31: 177–93.

Kamenka, E. and Krygier, M. (eds) (1979) *Bureaucracy*. London: Arnold.

Kaufman, H. (1981) Fear of bureaucracy: a raging pandemic. *Public Administration Review*, 41: 1–9.

Knei-Paz, B. (1978) *The Social and Political Thought of Leon Trotsky*. Oxford: Clarendon Press.

Lane, J-E. (ed.) (1987) *Bureaucracy and Public Choice*. London: Sage.

Lassman, P. and Speirs, R. (eds) (1994) *Weber: Political Writings*. Cambridge: Cambridge University Press.

Lefort, C. (1974) What is bureaucracy? *Telos*, 22: 31–65.

Lefort, C. (1986) *The Political Forms of Modern Society*. Cambridge: Polity Press.

Levin, M. (1983) Marxism and democratic theory, in G. Duncan (ed.) *Democratic Theory and Practice*, pp. 79–95. Cambridge: Cambridge University Press.

Lewin, L. (1991) *Self-interest and Public Interest in Western Politics*. Oxford: Oxford University Press.

Lindblom, C. (1977) *Politics and Markets*. New York: Basic Books.

Loewith, K. (1982) *Max Weber and Karl Marx*. London: Allen and Unwin.

Lukes, S. (1985) *Marxism and Morality*. Oxford: Oxford University Press.

Lynn, J. and Jay, A. (1983) *Yes Minister*, 3 vols. London: BBC Publications.

Mallet, S. (1974) *Bureaucracy and Technocracy in the Socialist Countries*. Nottingham: Spokesman Books.

Mandel, E. (1973) *On Bureaucracy: a Marxist Analysis*. London: New Left Books.

Mandel, E. (1979) Why the Soviet bureaucracy is not a new ruling class. *Monthly Review*, July–August: 63–76.

Mandel, E. (1992) *Power and Money: a Marxist Theory of Bureaucracy*. London: New Left Books.

Marris, R.L. (1964) *The Economic Theory of 'Managerial Capitalism'*. London: Macmillan.

Marx, K. (1968) The Eighteenth Brumaire of Louis Bonaparte and Critique of the Gotha Programme, in K. Marx and F. Engels, *Selected Works*, 1 vol., pp. 97–180 and 319–35. Moscow: Foreign Languages Publishing House.

Marx, K. (1970) *Critique of Hegel's 'Philosophy of Right'*. Cambridge: Cambridge University Press.

Marx, K. and Engels, F. (1971) *Writings on the Paris Commune*. Moscow: Foreign Languages Publishing House.

Merton, R.K. (ed.) (1952) *Reader in Bureaucracy*. Glencoe, IL: The Free Press.

Michael, J. (1982) *The Politics of Secrecy*. Harmondsworth: Penguin Books.

Michels, R. (1959) *Political Parties*. Glencoe, IL: The Free Press.

Miller, G.J. and Moe, T.M. (1983) Bureaucrats, legislators and the size of government. *American Political Science Review*, 77: 297–322.

Milward, H.B. and Rainey, H.G. (1983) Don't blame the bureaucracy! *Journal of Public Policy*, 3: 149–68.

Moe, T.M. (1984) The new economics of organization. *American Journal of Political Science*, 28: 739–77.

Moe, T.M. (1990) The politics of structural choice: toward a theory of public bureaucracy, in O.E. Williamson (ed.) *Organization Theory*, pp. 116–53. New York: Oxford University Press.

Mommsen, W.J. (1974) *The Age of Bureaucracy*. Oxford: Blackwell.

Mommsen, W.J. (1981) Max Weber and Roberto Michels. *Archives Européennes de Sociologie*, 22: 100–16.

Mommsen, W.J. (1989) *The Political and Social Theory of Max Weber: Collected Essays*. Cambridge: Polity Press.

Mouzelis, N.P. (1975) *Organization and Bureaucracy*, 2nd edn. London: Routledge.

Nadel, M.V. and Rourke, F.E. (1975) Bureaucracies, in F.I. Greenstein and N.W. Polsby (eds) *Handbook of Political Science*, vol. 5, pp. 373–440. Reading, MA: Addison-Wesley.

Nelkin, D. (1977) *Technological Decisions and Democracy*. London: Sage.

Niskanen, W.A. (1971) *Bureaucracy and Representative Government*. Chicago, IL: Aldine.

Niskanen, W.A. (1973) *Bureaucracy, Servant or Master?* London: Institute of Economic Affairs.

Nove, A. (1991) *The Economics of Feasible Socialism Revisited*. London: Allen and Unwin.

Nuti, D.M. (1992) Market socialism: the model that might have been but never was, in A. Aslund (ed.) *Market Socialism*, pp. 17–31. Cambridge: Cambridge University Press.

Ollman, B. (1977) Marx's vision of communism: a reconstruction. *Critique*, 8: 4–42.

Orzechowski, W. (1977) Economic models of bureaucracy, in T.E. Borcherding (ed.) *Budgets and Bureaucrats*. Durham, NC: Duke University Press.

Page, E.C. (1992) *Political Authority and Bureaucratic Power: A Comparative Analysis*, 2nd edn. Hemel Hempstead: Harvester Wheatsheaf.

Parkinson, C.N. (1958) *Parkinson's Law*. London: Murray.

Pateman, C. (1970) *Participation and Democratic Theory*. Cambridge: Cambridge University Press.

Perez-Diaz, J.M. (1978) *State, Bureaucracy and Civil Society*. London: Macmillan.

Perrow, C. (1972) *Organizational Analysis: a Sociological View*. London: Tavistock Publications.

Peters, B.G. (1977) Insiders and outsiders: the politics of pressure group influence on bureaucracy. *Administration and Society*, 9: 191–218.

Peters, B.G. (1981) The problem of bureaucratic government. *Journal of Politics*, 43: 56–82.

Peters, B.G. (1987) Politicians and bureaucrats in the politics of policymaking, in J.-E. Lane (ed.) *Bureaucracy and Public Choice*, pp. 255–82. London: Sage.

Peters, B.G. (1995) *The Politics of Bureaucracy*, 4th edn. White Plains, NY: Longman.

Piekalkiewicz, J. and Hamilton, C. (eds) (1991) *Public Bureaucracies Between Reform and Resistance*. Oxford: Berg.

Pierson, C. (1986) *Marxist Theory and Democratic Politics*. Cambridge: Polity Press.

Pierson, C. (1995) *Socialism After Communism*. Cambridge: Polity Press.

Polan, A.J. (1984) *Lenin and the End of Politics*. London: Methuen.

Pollitt, C. (1986) Democracy and bureaucracy, in D. Held and C. Pollitt (eds) *New Forms of Democracy*, pp. 158–91. London: Sage.

Ponting, C. (1986) *Whitehall: Tragedy and Farce*. London: Hamilton.

Ponting, C. (1990) *Secrecy in Britain*. Oxford: Blackwell.

Pressman, J.L. and Wildavsky, A.B. (1983) *Implementation*. Berkeley, CA: University of California Press.

Ranson, S. and Stewart, J. (1994) *Management for the Public Domain*. London: Macmillan.

Rattansi, A. (1982) *Marx and the Division of Labour*. London: Macmillan.

Riggs, F.W. (1964) *Administration in Developing Countries*. Boston, MA: Houghton.

Rizzi, B. (1985) *The Bureaucratization of the World*, trans. A. Westoby. London: Tavistock Publications.

Robertson, K.G. (1982) *Public Secrets*. London: Macmillan.

Rose, R. (1984) *Understanding Big Government*. London: Sage.

Roth, G. and Schluchter, W. (1979) *Max Weber's Vision of History*. Berkeley, CA: University of California Press.

Rowley, C.K. (ed.) (1993) *Public Choice Theory*, vol. 3. Aldershot: Elgar.

Rule, J.B. (1974) *Private Lives and Public Surveillance*. New York: Schochen.

Scaff, L. (1981) Max Weber and Robert Michels. *American Journal of Sociology*, 86: 1269–85.

Schluchter, W. (1981) *The Rise of Western Rationalism*. Berkeley, CA: University of California Press.

Schluchter, W. (1987) From government over persons to the administration of things: Marx and Engels on bureaucracy, in R.M. Glassman, W.H. Swatos and P.L. Rosen (eds) *Bureaucracy Against Democracy and Socialism*, pp. 11–30. Westport, CT: Greenwood Press.

Schumpeter, J.A. (1947) *Capitalism, Socialism and Democracy*. London: Allen and Unwin.

Self, P. (1972) *Administrative Theories and Politics*. London: Allen and Unwin.

Self, P. (1993) *Government by the Market? The Politics of Public Choice*. London: Macmillan.

Stivers, C. (1990) The public agency as polis: active citizenship in the administrative state. *Administration and Society*, 22: 86–105.

Subramaniam, V. (1990) Introduction, in V. Subramaniam (ed.) *Public Administration in the Third World*, pp. 1–14. Westport, CT: Greenwood Press.

Sweezy, P. (1979) Is there a ruling class in the USSR? *Monthly Review*, October and July–August: 1–17 and 76–86.

Thompson, D.F. (1980) The moral responsibility of public officials. *American Political Science Review*, 74: 905–16.

Thompson, D.F. (1983) Bureaucracy and democracy, in G. Duncan (ed.) *Democratic Theory and Practice*, pp. 233–50. Cambridge: Cambridge University Press.

Trotsky, L. (1972) *The Revolution Betrayed*. New York: Pathfinder Press.

von Mises, L. (1936) *Socialism*. London: Cape.

von Mises, L. (1944) *Bureaucracy*. New Haven, CT: Yale University Press.

Wade, L.L. (1979) Public administration, public choice and the pathos of reform. *Review of Politics*, 41: 344–74.

Weber, M. (1978) *Economy and Society*, 2 vols. Berkeley, CA: University of California Press. Especially pp. 217–26, 956–1005, and 1381–469.

Weber, M. (1978) Socialism, in W.G. Runciman (ed.) *Weber, Selections in Translation*, pp. 251–62. Cambridge: Cambridge University Press.

Williamson, O.E. (1975) *Markets and Hierarchies*. New York: Free Press.

Woodward, J. (1980) *Industrial Organization*, 2nd edn. Oxford: Oxford University Press.

Wright, E.O. (1978) *Class, Crisis and the State*. London: New Left Books.

Index